EVERYTHING WILL BE ALRIGHT

MY HEART WILL BEAT FOR YOU

EVERYTHING WILL BE ALRIGHT

MY HEART WILL BEAT FOR YOU

By Nayeli Pereznegrón Galindo

Translated by Alejandra Salazar.

Edited by Humberto Márquez.

www.eloquento.com

To Luis Pablo, with all my love.

ACKNOWLEDGEMENTS

Thank you, God, for giving me the most beautiful gift.

Luis Pablo, my *Pavito*, my little angel, my eternal love. You knew my heart better than anyone, and still do. Thank you for coming to this world to transform my heart and to help me discover what I am made of and what life is truly about.

Luis, my partner. Thank you for always believing in me and reminding me that I can do anything. For always supporting my dreams, for being part of them and embracing them as your own. For the enormous faith that you pass on to me every day. For your patience and never-ending love, which is totally reciprocated.

To my parents. Thank you for your love and patience that gave me these wings to help me fly and not fall. Because despite being "so different" you taught me to accept, love, and cherish myself without regrets. Thank you for helping me to make the most of my deep desire of not being like everyone else, of going against the flow, and changing my surroundings. Thank you for teaching me by example how to raise my voice among injustices and to always speak my mind.

To my sisters, thank you for your never-ending love for me and my kids. For your dedication, mindfulness, and patience in my darkest moments. For always finding the perfect excuse to be present.

Thank you to those who prayed for our family. We are standing here today because of your prayers.

Thank you to every single person that has been a part of LPAP A.C. For pouring your heart out in something I do for my own son. My admiration goes to you.

Thank you to so many people that for editorial reasons are not named in this book. That doesn't mean you don't have a special place in my heart. For your love, fellowship, friendship, support, love, commitment, and donations.

To those involved in making this book a reality. Goga, thank you for such beautiful pictures, for your advice, and good vibes. Anita, my former roommate, thank you for working so hard putting into words so many ideas and so much love. Fr. Jorge Obregón, who besides having a titanic mission, has made the time to guide and help me with mine, words will never express my gratitude and admiration for you. Alejandra Salazar, thank you for unselfishly translating so much love into another language and making sure it would pass on, thank you for your enormous contribution to this cause. To my family at Texas Children's Hospital, thank you for all your love, affection, and disposition, always. You are still in my prayers every day.

To you who are reading this book, thank you for supporting Luis Pablo's foundation and helping childhood cancer in lower income families. I am sure you will learn about a great life and love lesson in return. Enjoy it!

FOREWORD

Why? Why would you want to work with kids with cancer?

How? How can you work with kids that are dying?

Isn't there something else you can do that isn't so sad? These are typical questions I get when I tell people I am a pediatric oncology nurse. And honestly, I can understand why people ask the same questions each time. If you haven't spent time in the emotional roller-coaster world that is pediatric cancer, you couldn't possibly understand it. But now that I have, I couldn't imagine doing anything else.

These families, just like the story of the family you are about to read, are the most amazing people you will ever know. They will show you exactly what it means to live compassionately and without fear.

Matthew 18:3 says: "Truly, I say to you, unless you turn and become like children, you will never enter the Kingdom of Heaven." There is definitely something remarkable about the resilient spirit of a child, but, the spirit of child fighting cancer? That is something incomparable to anything else I have ever seen!

Luis Pablo was no different. He didn't care how exhausted he was from lack of sleep, how many times his Ommaya port in his scalp had been accessed to administer chemotherapy straight to his nervous system, or how many pokes he had that day, all he wanted to do was go to the playroom or have someone push him around the hospital floor in his car.

I watched Nayeli and Luis walk around the unit over and over again with red and exhausted eyes, but with a reassuring smile on their face anytime Luis Pablo looked back at them. I watched these two amazing people go through some of the most unimaginable heartbreak and suffering a parent can take, and not once did they lose sight of the role they played in making sure their sweet little boy never let cancer win. The strength they showed each and every day will stay with me forever, and will remind me what really matters during our time here on earth.

I miss Luis Pablo. I miss him so very much. He was one of those patients you couldn't help but fall in love with. He was a gorgeous little boy, had the sweetest smile and laugh, and could light up a room with his happy spirit. But there was something else, something more. I could never understand what it was that drew me to him and his family so strongly but I am so thankful God brought them to me. He was my first novio and I was so honored to be loved by him.

Stacy del Greco
Pediatric Oncology Nurse

I had the privilege of being Luis Pablo's nurse many times during the long months he and his family spent in the inpatient unit at Texas Children's Hospital. He is one of those patients that will remain in my heart forever and that changed the way I practice nursing.

One of the things I remember the most is how his parents used music to soothe Luis Pablo when we had to draw his labs, change his dressings, or during any procedure they knew would be painful for him. As soon as they would see us coming, dad would grab his guitar, and both mom and dad would start serenading Luis Pablo. Their voices would fill the room with love that was felt by Luis Pablo and everyone else in the room. His eyes would focus on his loving parents and we as nurses would do our task as fast as possible while he basked in the songs of love.

Even during the most difficult moments of his treatments, his parents were resolute to show him their love through their song. He knew he was so very loved. His eyes reflected that love to all who cared for him.

Since then, I sing to all my young patients when doing painful procedures in hopes that they are soothed by the melody, and in hopes that my love for them reaches their heart the way Luis Pablo's songs reached mine.

Melissa López
Luis Pablo's Nurse

I will always remember the very first time I met you, Luis, along with your parents. You were just such a little guy with the most beautiful smile.

You had a rough disease, Acute Myeloid Leukemia, and you had some very rough treatment! But I don't recall a day passing that you did not offer a smile. Your parents, grandparents, and other family members were by your side as you fought the toughest battle ever, a battle to save your life. It was so, so hard on your family but still… you never lost that sweet smile on your face. And how you loved a party, especially if Mickey Mouse was there!

You are in my heart daily and I know you are still smiling up there in Heaven waiting for all of us to join you one day. Your picture sits on my desk and it's the first thing I see each day when I come to my office, it's a picture celebrating your end of therapy. Sending all my love to you.

ZoAnn Dreyer
Luis Pablo's Oncologist

I will never forget their smiles.

When I first met Luis Pablo and his parents, it was their infectious smiles that struck me the most. Faced with a horrendous diagnosis for their son, the family expressed nothing but warmth and gratitude, their sadness showing through thankful smiling faces.

I was extraordinarily lucky to become one of the long term physicians caring for Luis Pablo when he was admitted to the hospital for his cancer treatments. Rounding on him daily became a treat, a time to play, to chat, to form a friendship. No matter the news I carried, Luis Pablo's family welcomed me into their room each day, and slowly welcomed me in into their lives.

Their room was a happy room. When bad news outweighed the good, I could see the family grow stronger, remaining positive and optimistic, never letting hope fail. Grandparents, aunts, and uncles all added to that strength, banding together and lifting Luis Pablo and his parents up onto their shoulders. The love and respect they all had for one another was a gift to witness.

When Luis Pablo passed away, I again saw their sad smiles, but this time there was a glimmer behind them. Although their infinite strength and love could not have saved their son, he had sparked something more in them, something bigger than any of us. This time, it was his strength and love pushing them forward, setting them on a path to help fight for as many children and families facing horrific cancer diagnoses as possible. In such darkness, this remarkable family again banded together and helped each other find a way out, find a way to the light, together.

Today, as I watch Luis Pablo's brother and sister grow up, I am again struck by their smiles. They are the smiles of children at peace, loved by their family both on Earth and in Heaven. And I am certain that Luis Pablo is smiling down upon them.

Ann Marshburn
Luis Pablo's physician

To know Luis Pablo was a gift, he had a smile for days.

I had the privilege of getting to know 'little man' when I was his nurse at Texas Children's hospital during his long battle with Acute Myeloid Leukemia. To this day, I still remember his unforgettable smile and a laugh that melted every heart!

My heart filled with joy every time I walked into Luis Pablo's room, and it also melted with sorrow as I witnessed the pain Luis Pablo and his parents, Luis and Nayeli, endured during his excruciating battle with cancer.

Luis Pablo was the star of the show every day. He had the entire nursing staff at Texas Children's Cancer Center requesting to take care of him each and every day. Everyone knew Luis

Pablo and even if he wasn't your assigned patient for the day you, couldn't wait to walk into his room.

Watching him toddle down the hallways, attached to his IV pole and waving at all he came into contact with, is a very fond memory that I will always cherish. Luis Pablo was a little man with a BIG personality who became a permanent imprint on my heart.
He was one in a billion and God requested his presence far too soon. I know Luis Pablo is the star in heaven and always smiling, and smiling! I love you Luis Pablo!

Danielle Johnston
Luis Pablo's Nurse

Driving that red car, full head of hair, smile on his face. It's impossible to forget that first image of Luis Pablo driving down the halls of Texas Children's Hospital.

If there is one lesson that LPAP and his family taught every one of us who worked at TCH, it is a lesson of love. Against all odds, they smiled, they laughed, they played with superheroes.

LPAP would cheer you up when you were down, he would make you smile when you were sad, you would leave happier than you were before you went into his room. Even during the hardest of days, the love Luis Pablo had inside, the love that Luis, Nayeli, and his entire family had to share, was inspiring in many ways.

Luis Pablo taught us lessons that you couldn't learn anywhere else. Lessons that stay for a lifetime.

Donald Thigpen
VAT Team member

CONTENTS

LUIS PABLO

Hello, my love,

Someone suggested I should write you and I think it is a good idea to tell you all about what we are going through right now, because I know you will be healthy one day and you will read about the miracle that God has granted us: YOUR LIFE FOR THE SECOND TIME.

I don't want to leave out anything that we are experiencing in this hospital. It is very easy to dismiss the bad moments when we are having a good one, but I don't want to forget all this suffering. I knew it existed, but I never imagined how hard it would be to face your own child's illness, or the amount of families that face adversity every day in this hospital. I don't get how I spent so many years thinking me and my family would never go through something as horrible as this. I thought I was untouchable, but boy, was I wrong!

I am quite the happy mom. My life changed completely when I found out I was pregnant. It was no longer me, it was us, and the love I felt by knowing you were growing inside me was something hard to describe. Every movement, every kick, every beat of your heart that was synchronized with mine created a bond that only a mother and child can have. You are a very loved baby, we longed for you so badly, my firstborn, the first boy in my family, we were all crazy for you.

Your birth was not an easy one. After 23 hours of labor, I spiked a fever and the doctors decided to do a c-section. The second I held you in my arms I knew you were going to be a fighter. We made a great team, and your dad was always by our side. Our family is filled with love and I am very proud of that.

As the months went by, I was more and more amazed by you with every day that passed. My whole life changed, I decided to grow closer to God. I was extremely grateful for having you in my life. You are a smart kid, full of peace and joy. The only thing you want to do is blow kisses to make other people smile. Your grandma kept saying you were special.

"Mom, he is your grandchild," I would say.

"No," she'd reply. "I don't say it because of that, I really think he is a *mystical* baby."

I enjoyed every second I spent with you when we were home, when you would come to work with me, when you played with your dad. You are my whole entire life and I cannot even imagine living without you.

Your first birthday was coming up, your first year of life and my first one as a mom! I felt so special and grateful for having a baby so full of light. I put all my love into planning your birthday party.

Luis Pablo's birthday party

I decided to have a harvest theme with pumpkins and scarecrows, but nothing too scary. You were born on October 29, just a couple of days before Halloween, a popular holiday in the northern part of Mexico because of its proximity to the United States. We had your party on Friday, November 1st so that your grandmother, aunts, and uncles could come all the way from León, Guanajuato.

I was in charge of every single thing and coordinated every detail. Your grandma would tell me there was no need for all of that since you were not going to remember anything, and she was probably right. But the memories of the party and the days leading up to it would be captured in pictures, and I wanted to show you those later so that you could see all the love and effort I put into planning your first birthday party.

Two days before your party, you had a fever. I thought it was a simple cold or virus because I was also feeling under the weather, but we both woke up with a very high temperature on the big day. I quickly started to get ready to go see your doctor in hopes that he would give us a magic remedy that would make us both feel better. Calling off your party was the last thing I would do. They gave us both a shot, and like magic we were soon feeling better, with no fever and ready to celebrate. Mission accomplished!

You knew the party was for you. You tried all the games and activities, had cake, hit the piñata, and smiled at all the costumes, including yours. I poured my heart into planning your party, and all the guests could tell.

The days went by and the fever would not go away. On New Year's eve, we were in Mexico City with our family ready to welcome 2014, when you suddenly started to shiver and complain in pain. Your dad immediately suggested we should go, I honestly thought it was just one more fever that would go away with some ibuprofen, but this time it was not like that. We asked one of my cousins to take us back to our hotel, but something happened on our way there that we got lost. All of a sudden, we were welcoming the new year in the middle of the road.

"Happy New Year!" my cousin said.

That was when I kissed your dad, and then you. The moment my lips touched your forehead I felt it burning. It was hot and sweaty, and for the first time, something inside me came to a halt. I consider myself an optimistic person, so I did not want to think that

Happy *New Year!*

something was wrong. I took a deep breath, got into our hotel room and stayed up all night trying to bring your fever down with wet cloths and medicine. The next morning we took you to the best hospital in the city. After they examined you, they told us the same thing we had heard before "It's just a virus, kids are always getting sick this time of the year." But that day, my heart did not feel at ease with that answer.

Back in Saltillo, Coahuila, the beautiful city we live in, land of the dinosaurs that is now filled with hickory trees, you started walking. We were so happy! The first steps of a whole life ahead. Roughly two months after your birthday, the fever came back and it would not go below 104 degrees Fahrenheit. I gave you medicine and cold baths, I rubbed alcohol on your feet and followed the doctor's recommendations. I tried every trick and advice I was given, with no luck.

Thank goodness -and my mom- I have always been cautious and even a little wary when it comes to a fever. I do this because when your aunt Ale (Aaii, as you call her,) was little, she got meningitis, which caused her permanent hearing loss. Again, we went to see your doctor, Marcelo Valdés, a great physician and wonderful human being. He examined you and ordered some blood work.

On Sunday, January 26, you did not wake up like always, asking for your milk. Ever since you were six months old, you have been sleeping for 12 hours every night, and like clockwork at 8 a.m. you demand your milk. It was nine o'clock and still no cries. Worried, I went to your room. You were awake and when you looked at me I could see the pain in your eyes. I lifted you up and felt your hair drenched in sweat, as if someone had poured a bucket of water on you. I touched your pillow and it was soaking wet, too. Scared, I called your dad for help, I asked him to go to the pharmacy to get more medicine. You could not even cry, the fever and excessive sweat had made you lethargic. Nothing would bring the fever down. A whole hour went by, an hour filled with silent moans that hurt in the deepest part of my being. I started praying to try to calm down my anxiety. Dad was taking too long, so I called him, upset.

"Where are you?" A long silence was the only response.

"Luis, are you there? Can you hear me?"

"Yes," he replied. He was crying.

"What's going on?" I asked. "Is everything okay?"

"I'm almost home, I'll tell you in a minute."

When he arrived I could tell he was crying, his face was red. He barely managed to say "sit down." Right there, I knew he was going to tell me something about the thing we loved the most.

"I'm not going to sit down, just tell me what's going on!"

"The pediatrician called," he said.

"What is wrong with our baby?" I hurried him.

"He wants us to go to his office."

"On a Sunday? Something must be very wrong," I thought to myself.

"It's leukemia."

A long silence took over.

"We're going to fight this *chaparrita*, we're going to get over this, you'll see!" Your dad tried to comfort me as a thousand tears ran down my face.

"There's no time to lose," was the first thing that came to my mind.

Still crying, I started to get ready to leave, and as I was fixing your beautiful hair it hit me: I could not believe you had leukemia.

My whole life flashed before my eyes. I felt the blood go to my feet. I remembered the struggle and pain I felt during your birth. I saw the memories of my wedding day. I remembered when my sister got sick. I cried, I was mad, and I was angry at God. I acted like any mother would do when she hears such disturbing news about her child. Your father, on the other hand, was always calm and quiet, accepting God's will, confident in a miracle.

My recollection of the rest of the day is just a blur. We went to the doctor's office and learned more about your illness. The doctor told us to have faith and he referred us to an oncologist in Monterrey, Nuevo León, a neighboring city.

"Jesus, I trust in You!" your pediatrician said as we were leaving. I took those words to heart, engraving them in my mind and in my soul.

When we got home, I gave you a bath and I got in your crib with you. I have never done that before. It is a very special crib. Your grandfather had it specially made when he found out he was having a grandson. It is a beautiful crib, but not the most comfortable for an adult. Somehow I managed to get in and I held you. As you fell asleep right next to me, I thought about a movie your dad and I had watched around Christmas. It was based on a true story about a boy and his family's fight against leukemia. When the movie was over, I could not stop crying. I had never been so emotional about a movie. I was thinking about you and the simple thought of you getting sick would make me shake. Your dad hugged me and asked why I was crying so much.

"I don't know, we're very lucky. God has given us so much, Luis," I replied. "We have to ask for His guidance to learn how we can be of help to show gratitude for all that we have."

I shuddered recalling that memory. The only thing I could say was: "God, I don't want your guidance anymore, I get it, I'm going to help others, but please don't mess with my son."

That Monday I could not sleep, I felt numb, as if I was having a bad dream. We arrived at the oncologist's office in Monterrey, and he immediately ordered more tests, almost confirming the diagnosis. That was when our long torment began, trying to find blood and platelet donors because your levels were decreasing. We started to do some team work in order to find them.

The first thing I did was post on social media. Posts were shared by our friends and acquaintances, and we got responses very quickly. People from Monterrey that we did not know started coming into the clinic just for the sake of helping you. Donors from Saltillo also traveled to Monterrey to help you.

I think of social media as a miracle, I don't know what I would have done without it. It is hard to imagine what people did before in situations like these. How would they find so many donors? There is no doubt that social media has lightened up the load for us.

One of my cousins also helped us find more donors. Through her work, she was able to contact some members of the Mexican Army living in Monterrey, and they also donated blood and platelets for you. You see? Now your veins are carrying blood from many soldiers, I am sure this is a sign that everything will be fine.

Nayeli Pereznegrón
January 26, 2014

It breaks my heart to see my Luis Pablo sick! But he hasn't lost his charm, silliness, or joy. He teaches me so much!!!

👍 41   💬 18   ➤

Nayeli Pereznegrón
January 27, 2014

They just admitted my baby to the hospital, we don't have a clear diagnosis yet but he is in a delicate state of health. I'm a firm believer in the power of prayer. Please keep him in your prayers!!! The more we pray, the more we'll be heard!!!!

👍 289   💬 103   ➤

After you had a blood and platelets transfusion, the doctor explained we needed to do a lumbar puncture to confirm the diagnosis and to know which foods you needed to avoid. The procedure was scheduled for Thursday.

I prayed a rosary while they did the puncture. I was stressed and anxious to get the results. I tried to trick myself thinking the tests would show something different, a lot of people were praying for you and waiting on an update. I was impressed to see so many people impacted by you, praying for a miracle. Friends of mine put together prayer meetings, they organized Holy Hours and Masses. Your best friend's mom, auntie Maryjose, was the one who started and promoted all this prayer.

María Jose César
January 27, 2014

Luis Pablo is the son of Luis Aguilar and Nayeli Pereznegrón de Aguilar. He's a beautiful 15-month-old baby. He's a joyful, loving, smiling, very very happy and very special little boy. He has a unique charm that fills all of us who know him with happiness and joy.

We are asking for your prayers. Right now they're performing a very delicate procedure on him and we know that the more people that pray together, our Mary Mystical Rose and Our Lord will intercede for Luis Pablo's health and for his family. Let us pray so that Mary covers them with her mantle during these difficult times and may She hold them through every step of this trial.

👍 339 💬 7 ➔

Having the support and prayers of so many people helped us come to peace and to be confident while waiting on the results. It is only now that I am going through something so difficult that I understand the power a prayer holds. The power of prayer, Luis Pablo, is amazing. When you are so desperate and you feel like you cannot take it anymore, pray, and you will see how amazing things happen. Praying is talking God's language, and even if I used to think that when I was praying I was just saying the same thing over and over again, now that I am going through this... I get it.

The results were in and they brought many emotions. To my surprise, the doctor said there were no cancerous cells in your marrow. He called it a special case. When everything indicated leukemia, the most accurate test could not prove it.

"It's a miracle!" I said. "There's a lot of people praying."

He was not very convinced, though. He told us to wait and asked us to be patient. Every day he would order more blood work, and every day the outlook of it being an early detection of leukemia was clearer.

Meanwhile, I would collapse with every result and agonize again like the first time we heard the news. I had gotten my hopes up with the lumbar puncture results, I had seen a light nearby, I filled my mind with positive thoughts. "It's not going to be leukemia!" I would say to myself. But then I saw every other test result get worse, and I was getting used to the idea of this illness. I did this only from seeing the test results, because you are still the same, you sleep a little more but you laugh, dance, blow kisses, make the sign of the Holy Cross, and play. You are a regular child, and you show no sign of that horrible illness. Maybe this is the way God is working his miracle on us, by not letting us see you in pain.

I just want you to be healed, I don't care how long the road is. I will always be right here to walk by your side, together with your daddy and God until we reach the top. I love you, Luis Pablo! God really outdid Himself when He picked you as our son. I am so lucky to be your mother and my only wish is that this nightmare is soon over and that we can be back home enjoying life and your childhood.

I love you with all my heart, and like I always ask you: "How does my heart beat for you?" By the way, your dad was the one who came up with that phrase, but he later let me use it as mine.

"Bum, bum, bum, bum," you tell me in such a cute and naive way that my whole soul fills with the hope that our hearts will always beat like this, in sync and with joy, forever and ever.

Yesterday, I was so worn out and I could not write. They took you in for the procedure at 3 p.m. Both times I have been by your side when they put you to sleep. I imagine you are sleeping peacefully but it is a nightmare for me. Watching how my little piece of heaven is so vulnerable to this white liquid that immediately makes you sleep. Watching you fall asleep so fast smashes my soul. Putting you to sleep today was traumatic, even more than the first time, you cried really hard when they poked you and I was not able to make you laugh so that you were happy when you fell asleep.

It was a long procedure. After two hours of waiting the doctor came out, he was jumpy and excited.

"It was a though one!" He said.

He explained that because you are so little, your bones are not completely formed and they were only finding cartilage. But they needed to get a sample of your bones to do a biopsy and determine if you have leukemia. To get to your marrow they had to puncture both sides of your pelvis, and finally, your shinbone like last time.

You were crying really hard when you came out, you were out of control. We went to your room and you had your bottle, it was almond milk since we have banned all dairy because they feed cancer cells. You gobbled it up! That was why you were so cranky, you had been fasting since 7 a.m.

I can't stay in the corner, I can't say I don't want to see him cry because then, who will? Who will watch him cry? I need to be strong for him!"

I am 26 years old, and while my friends are busy making plans for the weekend, I stay up late learning about a possible leukemia that I might have to face with my first and only child. I have been very stressed out and that is why yesterday I flew off the handle. We need to stay strong as a family! I know it is not easy to understand, only a mom who has gone through this would be able to get it. Just as we hang on and are strong for our children, we need the grandparents to be strong for us, it is a chain of strength.

I know we all deal with things in different ways, and my dad is having a hard time with this because his heart is bigger than his head, it always weighs on him more. I used to be like that, but as they say "What doesn't kill you makes you stronger," and with this illness I have learned to become stronger to be able to comfort you.

Your grandpa is my pillar of strength, but sometimes I wish he just hugged me, like he did when I was a little girl and I knew no problem was ever big enough, because he would always protect me. Sometimes I feel so helpless that I want someone else to make all the decisions for me. Other times, I am overwhelmed with sorrow and desperation for not being able to solve all the issues we are facing. It is the sorrow of learning that nothing, my boy, absolutely nothing is under our control.

The day is finally over. A new day makes me so happy because it means hope, especially when the last day was so horrible. After a really bad night, the next day you were happy, eating, and playing, but when I went to change your diaper I noticed some of your stool had gotten into your wound. I ran to call the doctor and he quickly ordered to have your bandage removed without any sedatives. You cried so hard! I am learning to be a shelter for you when you are in pain. I hope that tomorrow will be a better day. Tomorrow we will have the results. There is a little light inside of me that believes you will soon be okay and that in a few short weeks we will be back in our house playing in the room that with so much love we decorated for you.

I love you. YOU ARE STRONG. And, how does my heart beat for you?

Today has been the worst day of my life. No doubt. You woke up with a fever and in pain. Early in the morning your doctor told us he already had the results. As soon as he arrived at the hospital, he met me and your dad to let us know his suspicions were right. Your bone biopsy showed cancerous cells. Things had changed now, leukemia was no longer the doctor's priority, it was another type of cancer. I thought I was ready to hear the news, for two weeks I had mentally prepared myself for a leukemia diagnosis, but then again, you can never be ready for this kind of news.

I could not hold back my tears. My world collapsed, you are my whole world and you were about to face an enormous battle. Why? How? When did this happen? So many people were praying! We asked God to protect you!

I feel defeated and so, so sad, but it makes me happy to know that our families from León and Mexico City are by our side. They came just to give us a hug, some of them are just here for the day, taking the first flight in the morning and leaving that same night. We are very lucky to have such a tightknit family.

People from Saltillo also came to visit. Former classmates that I haven't seen since middle school came to donate blood and platelets. My sisters' friends, my parents' friends, my friends' friends. I never imagined there were so many people in the world willing to help. This is definitely something to learn from and to be

Luis Pablo's surgery

thankful for. When all this is over and we are out of the hospital, I will be the first in line when they are looking for donors.

Nayeli Pereznegrón
February 2, 2014

God is working and we can see it. Thank you for your prayers!

🖒 233   💬 11   ➔

Nayeli Pereznegrón
February 2, 2014

We got all the platelets we needed! Thank you so much!!

🖒 120   💬 3   ➔

I have to confess that amid all the stress and pain, one thought that I cannot seem to get out of my head is: "Why does your dad have to face this hard ship? Why him if he is such a nice and kind-hearted person? So devoted to you, God. Why him when he already lost his own father and has gone through so many sad and hard times with his family? Why his son now?"

And you know what the most amazing thing is? That he doesn't complain or protest. He only says that everything will be all right, that God is going to help us because He will never leave us, and I want to believe him so bad but there are moments when I cannot feel God. I refuse to believe there is a God that would allow this much pain on a child that has never hurt anybody and that only wants to be like any other kid his age. I know that this is not the truth and I want you to always love God, but today I just feel like he abandoned me. I feel so alone.

The doctor determined you needed more lab work because it seems like your heart is not doing so well. I was shattered, I was crying inconsolably with my mom in the waiting room.

"I can't stand this anymore!" I sobbed.

"Have faith sweetie," a lady that was sitting nearby gently said. "God does not abandon us."

Her husband, a man that seemed full of peace, encouraged me with tears in his eyes.

"Ask God for strength," he added. "Don't let go of his hand no matter how hard things get. If you're weak you won't be able to endure this. God is with you and we will pray for your son."

I was amazed at how God was using them to talk to me, and right there I made a commitment to always pray for the families that are suffering in hospitals.

As you know, there are a lot of people praying for you. I went on Facebook today and I looked for the group aunties Maryjose and Rocío created for you. For the first time ever, from the bottom of my heart, I asked for prayers. It was the only thing I could do, pray and invite others to do the same.

In less than 24 hours, the prayer group doubled its size. There were over a thousand people praying for you. I am sure God will hear us! People that had never prayed before started doing so when they heard your story. People that were not consistent with their prayers were now praying every single day because of you. You are working miracles, kiddo! You are an inspiration to many and I know God has big plans for you, never forget that. Close your eyes and ask yourself what is God expecting from you. Remember to always be grateful for this trial and to show your gratitude with actions. You are special and destined to be a great leader, and I am so proud to be the one who walks besides you.

Now off to wait for more results, to find out what type of cancer you have and how we will treat it. You have been here for 15 days already, one step at a time, but it seems like forever! I am very impatient. On top of that, God is testing my patience. It is so hard to have patience these days! But I do my best and my patience is my offering because I want your health back. I love you with all my heart and my soul, my dear beloved child!

Another day went by and we still have no official diagnosis. The doctor is not able to give one because the biopsy sample was not large enough. We decided to see another renowned oncologist in Monterrey for a second opinion, who without batting an eye said:

"Your son has no cancer, what he has is another disease in his blood."

"How can this be?" I asked. "His pediatrician and oncologist both agree that he has cancer, they just haven't found out where."

"That's not even possible," the doctor replied. It seemed like he was talking about politics or a tedious subject while talking about you.

"It's very simple," he added. "That doctor says your son has cancer, I say he doesn't. Who do you want him to be treated by? It's your call."

We immediately asked him to leave the room. We are not some kids playing doctor with our dolls. I cannot believe his lack of ethics and the size of his ego. I will not take this behavior towards such a delicate matter. This is why we have decided to treat you in a hospital in Houston. Your dad arranged everything for you to be admitted.

Telling your doctor we were leaving was not easy. He said he was close to figuring out what was wrong with you, but we could not wait any longer. We needed and wanted to give you the very best, and if the very best was on the other side of the world, we would take you there.

Our experience in Monterrey did not end well. The doctor who always said your health was fragile and banned visitors because it was too risky for you to see other people, refused to sign the insurance paperwork when he found out we were taking you to Houston. We needed that form in order to fly you in an air ambulance.

On Friday, February 14, while everybody was celebrating Valentine's Day, we were on our way to Houston. The doctor ordered one last blood and platelet transfusion so that you would be safe on the way there. Your transfer to Houston was a gift from a friend since the doctor did not agree to sign the authorization. We were still trying to figure out a way to take you there, when an angel called to let us know we had a plane waiting for us. You were perfectly fine and we will always be grateful for that.

Nayeli Pereznegrón
February 14, 2014

On this special day, we would like to say thank you all for your friendship and love. There are not enough words to express our gratitude for your support and prayers. Thank you for offering us your friendship through your prayer, whether we've met before or not. A friend of mine sent me this text (see? I read everything!) and I want to share it with you because it describes perfectly what we're experiencing right now.

During biblical times, when there were battles, Moses would pray for those that were fighting. He had to keep his arms up while he prayed, if he were to lower them, his people would lose strength, so he mustn't bring his arms down, ever. When he was tired and felt he could no longer go on, there were people that would hold his arms up while he continued praying.

We're like that, rising our arms for our child's battle, and you, our friends and family, holding our arms up with your support, encouraging messages, presence, prayers, love, and help. From the bottom of our hearts, thank you! Happy Valentine's Day! #lpap

Here's a little thank you smile from Luis Pablo.

👍 1 mil   💬 61   ➤

32

HOUSTON

We arrived on time. The ambulance was already waiting for you, I had never been in one before. I was scared, and on top of that I was in another country.

We arrived to the emergency room at Texas Children's Hospital. There, I saw a girl that I will never forget, because seeing her face was disturbing. A pale and swollen face that showed all her veins. Your grandma and I looked at each other and the only thing I could think of was "Thank you, God, because that is not my child." You never know how blessed you really are until you are in places like this. Many times I have thanked God because it is just cancer.

In the waiting room, we spent six hours filling out paperwork and answering questions. This hospital has a designated floor for every pediatric specialty and they told us you would be admitted to the 10th floor: Neurology. The decorations are lively. The rooms and hallways show real "works of art" made by children that have stayed there before. The floor (the thing that you see the most after hearing bad news) is very colorful. The nurses are kind and always smiling. It seems as if everything is pure happiness. Your room is small and the food is terrible. It is hard to believe that a hospital that specializes in cancer treatments would serve its patients microwave food. Luckily, we did not stay there too long. After some more tests, they moved us to the 9th floor.

Walking the halls of our new floor, I could see the signs on some of the doors. Two in particular made an impression on me: "We love you Savanah," and "You did it. Congratulations on your last chemo!" One of the rooms had a half-closed door and I could see a pale, extremely thin, bald little boy with dark circles under his eyes. "Welcome to oncology!" I thought.

I felt chills and I asked God to give me strength. I turned to see your grandma and she was crying. While being so strong all the time and without understanding the language, she could feel the uncertainty in those hallways, where the air is so cold that you feel it in your bones and where the hospital smell is way stronger because of all the chemicals they use.

The nurses then showed us an area with food and drinks available for the families.

"Because you are going to be here a long time," they said. Something you never want to hear.

During the day, grandma and I were depressed. We did not know what to expect, how long we would be in this room, if we would be back to our dear country soon, or even worse, if you would come back with us. A lot of things went through my mind, I was hopeless, an overwhelming sorrow had taken over me.

The next day, everything went back to normal. I was calmer and I thought: "Don't get ahead of yourself, miracles do happen, you don't know how long you'll be here, and if you need to stay here for years, you will do that for your son. You decide if you want to be happy or unhappy, Nayeli, how dramatic do you want your story to be?"

I took a deep breath and woke you up with my best smile. Right now, you are here with me and nothing is better than that! I have my husband, my mom, and you. I am very lucky and one of God's favorite children. He has sent me all this support to endure this pain, a lot of people go through much worse on their own. That was when I decided I was going to enjoy my days like I did outside the hospital. If you are this happy and smile all the time, I cannot fail you. Just like you always do your best, I will do my best too! I promise we will be happy here, Luis Pablo, I give you my word, I will make sure of it.

I grabbed a map and guide to the hospital to get to know all the places and plan some activities. I told you all about it: a room to watch TV, a kitchenette, and a computer room. On Tuesdays, they have a puppet show; on Sundays, a volunteer comes and plays the guitar. I wrote down all the events because I did not want you to miss anything. And then, I found a playroom! I quickly asked if I could take you there, but the doctor said no because you are having a procedure tomorrow. I promise I will take you there soon.

We entered the operating room at 11 a.m. This time, dad and I were there with you, they put you to sleep faster than usual. I hate seeing how they sedate you, it hurts me to my core when you start to close your eyes until you are unconscious. This time we did not have to wait as long as the previous two times. When you woke up, you were singing and dancing as if nothing had happened, everything is different in this hospital. I am grateful because we get to be here and I can see you feel better so quickly after a procedure, it is clear that all the little things make a big difference between this hospital and the last one.

At night they had to give you more medicine because you were complaining, your wound was bleeding a little but the doctors said that was normal. What was not normal is that the next day you walked all the way to the playroom! You played, danced, stood up, and even crawled. They had just made a puncture on both sides of your pelvis, you should be in pain, but once again, you surprised us.

On Thursday, February 20, we met the oncologist who was taking over your case, Dr. ZoAnn Dreyer, a woman who is hard to forget, not only because she can treat, heal, and help cancer patients, but because she is also an attractive blonde lady who dresses classy and fashionably. She is a celebrity around the hospital. She patiently explained that you have Acute Myeloid Leukemia M7 subtype with fibrosis, the most aggressive form of leukemia. Bad news.

Tears started running down my face, your dad held my hand. For a moment I went blank, until the following words echoed in my head: bone marrow transplant.

"What? Why? Is it completely necessary?" I asked.

The truth is nobody knows, it all depends on the results of your first chemo cycle. If you do well we probably won't need it, but the doctor stressed that with this type of leukemia, many of the patients require the transplant. I haven't looked into it that much, I don't know why but that word scares me so much, just like I used to be terrified by the words leukemia or cancer.

With such a quick and precise diagnosis, we knew we had to stay in Houston. Your dad quickly made arrangements to find an apartment and get everything I might need. My parents and sisters started taking turns and arranging their schedules to come and help us. They are the best, I don't know what we would do without them.

The next day, you had your first chemo at 5 a.m., and your second one just 12 hours later at 5 p.m. This will continue for the whole round and it might last up to 18 days, or maybe even more.

Nayeli Pereznegrón
February 21, 2014

Hello! We are asking for your prayers because my baby is starting a chemo treatment that will last 18 days. Then, he'll have a three day break and will continue with another round of chemotherapy just as aggressive. And we will have to do this for a while.

The first round is the most important. If he responds well to chemo, the diagnosis would take a positive turn. He has one of the most complex types of leukemia, that's why he needs such an aggressive treatment, but as I wrote yesterday: "Aggressive disease and treatment needs aggressive prayer." I'll share with you a short prayer that you start praying on a Friday, and then pray for 15 days straight. It's very miraculous and it'll help us greatly during this first round.

I want to share something that I've learned after a month of living in hospitals and experiencing all these feelings, something I hold deep in my heart: God is our Father, He is love, and just like parents want the best for our children, I firmly believe that He is not making bad things happen for us… evil exists, for example, cancer is a mutation that resulted after so many man-made changes done to nature, all the chemicals, our diet, whatever you want to call it, and sadly we're now facing this not because He picked us for this battle, not because we have a mission or because we're strong, but because evil exists and nobody is immune to that. The ONLY thing we can do is decide who to lean on, and who to trust. When you decide to surrender to God, the load is lighter. Without Him, I couldn't be so strong like you all say that I am. On the other hand, the good things that we have, those are because of God, and among those good things are the people who started this group and all of those who have joined, and the many, many, many, prayers.

A month ago we started a very difficult journey, thank God today we know how to fight back and we will do it with everything we've got. Thank you! And please don't stop praying for Luis Pablo!

The first day was the worst. All those chemicals were not kind to your body. You were irritable, you did not want to be touched, you cried easily, and you threw up twice. Your body fluids are tainted by toxic substances from the chemotherapy, the nurses told me I have to wear gloves and a coat when I hold you.

"Think about your future, not doing this could be harmful," one of them said.

"The only thing I have right now is my present," I replied. "If I was going through this, I wouldn't want my mom using gloves to touch me or talking to me with a face mask. Thank you, but I'm not doing that."

On day two, *Tata* (as you call your grandpa) arrived, and since then and up until today (day 7) you have been doing great. You dance, laugh, play, and eat. Of course nothing is like it used to be, but I am very proud of you, you are one brave baby, a fighter, a strong child, and a happy one. You are all of those things, and I remind you of that every night when you are sleeping. We are going to get through this, I am sure. Your grandpa stayed in the hospital with you every night so that your grandma and I could get some rest.

Being in the hospital is exhausting. Since you started chemo we have to change your diaper every two hours because the toxins in your urine could burn your skin. This could be dangerous because of your weakened immune system and a simple wound could be fatal or send us to the ICU, which terrifies me. I feel so much pressure because you depend on me, I am scared of doing something wrong that could hurt you, and I am so prone to making mistakes, I am not eating right or getting enough sleep, the stress makes me forget everything, I have a thousand reminders on my phone but sometimes I even forget to charge it. My only hope is that this will all end soon. Every day I ask God for the physical and emotional strength I need to be here.

Thank God I have my mom here, just like you have me. She might be more worn out but she is fighting right here with us. She decided she will be splitting her time between Houston and Saltillo. She will spend two weeks here with us, and two with your grandpa and aunts.

You know what, Luis Pablo? Joining forces is worth it, because we get the privilege of enjoying you, being with you every day is a gift.

Being in Houston has given us the chance to get to know our extended family that lives in the city and they have been looking after us, just like many friends and family that come to help when my mom goes back to Saltillo. Any and Leonardo are an enormous blessing, he is always willing to be a donor. A lot of people are worried and praying for us. I know this because on your Facebook group inbox there are over 500 messages, I haven't been able to read them all, but the ones I have seen are mostly people asking how you are doing.

Two days ago I cried like I have never cried before. Dr. Dreyer told us you are doing great, but that she is still considering the marrow transplant. I have done some research on the subject and it seems like finding a match is quite complicated. Finding platelet donors is hard enough, I cannot imagine how hard it will be to find somebody to donate bone marrow. I was dying to talk to your dad about my anguish, but he is working like crazy right now because our expenses are so high, I would rather not give him any more worries.

My anxiety got worse when I heard the little boy in the room next door had passed away, he had the same type of leukemia as you. He was a sweet boy with a tired demeanor, but with a special spark in his eyes. It seemed like he was fighting for something that he knew he was going to lose. Whenever I saw him, it made me think he did not want to give up because he wanted to enjoy the love from his mom a little more. It was like a gift from a very sick child to his devoted mother.

I locked myself in the bathroom because I needed to cry, and right there I was flooded with doubt. Ever since we got here I have been thinking about the things we will do when you are out of the hospital, and for the first time I asked myself: "What if he never gets out?" My whole body was shaken by this horrible anguish that only a mother can feel when thinking about losing a child. I had not thought about what we are really fighting against. Today, I understood, we are fighting against death!

I cannot imagine going through what the mother of the boy next door is experiencing right now. What would I do without my beautiful baby that gives me life? What would I do without those bright eyes and that smile that make my heart flutter? I need you with me, Luis Pablo! Forever! Please, never leave me, I am never going to leave you. Stay here with me, I have a lot of love to give you, a whole world for you to see, so many things that we will learn together. I love you with all my heart, never forget that.

Yesterday you had a fever. That same morning Dr. ZoAnn said:

"Wow! We're so lucky that he hasn't had any side effects, usually all kids start having a fever by the third day."

"My boy is not just any boy, he's special," I answered.

At 4 p.m. you were leaning against the window looking at the cars go by.

"Vroom, vroom… Mom, mom! Vroom," you were saying excited.

You looked so cute that I ran to give you a hug. I could feel you were warm, so I checked your temperature and it read 104. I worried and called the nurses. The doctors prescribed some antibiotics before waiting on the blood test results. In situations like these, they cannot wait to find out if the fever is caused by a bacteria or a virus. The staff keeps telling me this is normal, that every kid can have an infection caused by their own saliva or gastric juice, but I cannot help but feel hopeless and angry at myself, we have taken such good care of you and we have been so careful. Your grandma is always cleaning, she is so meticulous! It is horrible when you cannot control the uncontrollable.

Tomorrow you were supposed to have an intrathecal chemo, but they had to postpone it because of your fever. Now I understand why whenever I asked how long the treatment would take, they would always say: "We don't know for sure, sometimes things take a bad turn when the immune system is weak and that makes everything go slower."

I don't want to make friends in this place. You meet other moms in the family room, they are all fighters and have dark circles under their eyes, I have dark circles under my eyes too, but I try to put some make up on or I would be even more depressed. At first, I tried to fit in and make small talk, but I decided I don't want to do it, because the conversations were only about horrible things that could happen to you. I do not judge them, everyone deals with pain in different ways, but I cannot sit there listening to this pessimistic talk. It hurts me, it makes me suffer, it makes me feel hopeless. That is why I only greet them and quickly leave the room.

Luis Pablo, you have become my best friend. You are the only person I talk to, I know you cannot understand me, but I tell you everything and you only smile and rub my head while I lay next to you. Thank you for always listening without judgement.

41

You finally went one full day fever-free. This means tomorrow they will do a spinal tap and you will have your last chemo of the first cycle. You are so strong! You withstood two daily doses of chemo for 10 days. Now, we will start to see your globules, granulocytes, and hemoglobin counts go down. Once they go back up, we will begin your second round of chemo.

And, how does my heart beat for you?

Yesterday you were the same old happy kid. Your grandma and aunt came to visit. I think you were showing off how strong you are because you were standing up on your crib and moving your hips from one side to the other, as if you were trying to dance, and you were laughing!

We visited the playroom today. You have therapy every three days because after the first chemo round, you lost the strength in your legs. You used to be able to run, and now you cannot even walk. You are afraid to fall down. It has been a long process but I know this too shall pass.

Your dad will get here on Thursday, and on Friday we will both get our bone marrow tested. I hope we don't need it, but if we do, I want to be a match for you, my baby. If I could be the one in that bed hooked to all those machines I wouldn't hesitate to do it. I would love that things were different for you.

Speaking of your dad, I miss him so much. As a couple, things haven't been easy. Sometimes it is hard to find a moment to connect, but everything we are doing is worth it because we have you here with us. I long for the day when we can go back to the real world and be a regular family. For now, all we talk about is you and all things related. I miss him and it is awful to miss him while he is next to me. I know he misses me too, but we understand this is just a stage that will soon be over. I ask God to keep us together because we might have to face more challenges that will not be easy. Anyway, I will write again when we have any updates.

—◡♡2◡—

Dad and I got tested to find out if we are your match, and I am begging God that one of us is. I am a scaredy-cat when it comes to these things, but how would the mother of a child with cancer would look being frighten by a needle after all the things her child goes through? So I did it. I think my stress did not help, they were having trouble getting a good sample and they poked me three times. It hurt quite a bit and I was feeling guilty thinking of you.

Daddy left already. It was lovely having him here for a few days. He has no idea how much I miss him! You get so happy when you see him, it seems like you get pumped up with vitamins and forget any pain or complaint, you only want to be with him and play! He spent the night with you at the hospital and the two of you played a lot. I get a big relief when he is with us, I feel safe and lighter when he shares the load. A volunteer stopped by today to sing "Hero" by Enrique Iglesias and your dad cried.

Luis Pablo and his parents at a play corner in his hospital room.

Sometimes it is very hard to hold back our tears. We love you with all our hearts and we want to see you healthy.

And, how do our hearts beat for you?

Your cough woke me up in the middle of the night. It had only been half an hour since the nurse last came in. I stood up still half asleep.

"Come on Luis Pablo, the last thing we need right now is for you to get a cold, please don't get a cold, I'm so tired," I told you.

I don't know why I said that, as if it was your fault. I believe it was my exhaustion doing the talking. I immediately regretted saying that and I ran to hug you. I found some hair on your pillow, I touched your fine brown hair and it fell off on my hands. I felt an overwhelming pain in my chest and my eyes filled with tears. "How I wish it was just cold," I thought.

The cough was due to the hair that was falling off and landed on your pillow. I am so glad you don't notice that! You don't care about it, but I cannot help but feel sorrow, I would rather shave your head now to avoid the pain of seeing locks of your hair fall off every day. Besides, you

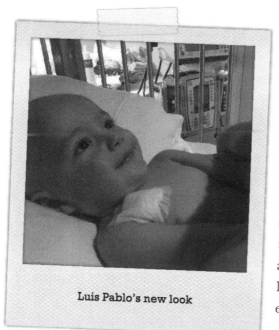

Luis Pablo's new look

44

keep saying "Mom, gross, hairs!" and you cough from all the hair that gets in your mouth. Oh well! I knew this was going to happen but I am not ready. But when have I been ready for any of the things that are happening now?

"Everything will be alright," you told me.

"Yes, baby, everything is going to be okay! I love you with all my heart. And, how does my heart beat for you?"

"Bum, bum, bum, bum," you answered with that spark in your eyes as a smile started to work its way across your face.

I held you closely and I told myself ten times: "Everything will be alright, Nayeli, everything is going be okay, one day at a time."

These last few months you have been hooked to the machine that provides medicine and nutrients 24/7. Although we can get used to anything, we were getting tired of hearing the beep and fighting the twisted cables at night when you turn on your side or when you want to stand up. You have been eating and drinking well so the doctors agreed to unplug you from 9 a.m to 5 p.m. That made you so happy! Now you can walk, crawl, and play comfortably, without pulling your catheter, you are the best! I overheard the nurses saying "the happiest little boy's room," they are all amazed at how happy you are.

I have to tell you that our next-door neighbor just found a matching donor for her daughter. God listened! They moved her to the 8th floor today where she will have her transplant. She deserves it, I am so happy for her, she is an immigrant and has been fighting for her daughter's life without speaking any English. Every time she needs something she has to call an interpreter. These days, if she notices we're not too busy, she looks for me and I go to her room to translate to make things go a little faster. You know what, son? I have learned to look into people's eyes and figure out many things. Remember to always look straight and into the eyes, they will tell you their story. The eyes of an immigrant are filled with desire, hope, and fear. I really admire them.

Dad and grandma had to go back to Saltillo, and now I am left alone with you. I cannot complain, but it is extremely tiring. The "robot" is beeping all night long, that is what we call the machine that pumps your chemotherapy. We added eyes and hands to it after you once pulled the cables and almost pulled out your catheter. I explained it was your friend, your best friend, and that he doesn't like being in this hospital either, but he does it for you, he wants you to get better, that is why he is always standing next to you and

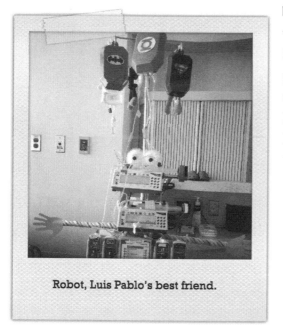

Robot, Luis Pablo's best friend.

letting the nurses know when your medicine is low. Since then, you pet him, talk to him, and sing with him. I have even started to like him and I talk to him sometimes too, he is our new best friend. At night, his beeps and having to change your diaper every two hours keep me awake and that makes me tired during the day.

46

Yesterday, guilt took over me. It was the middle of the night and I was exhausted. As I was changing your diaper I told you:

"Luis Pablo, give me five minutes, I just need five more minutes and we'll do something."

"Okay," you said.

I dozed off, until I heard your voice screaming: "Mom, mom, mom!" I stood up but my legs were pulling me back to the couch.

I went to the bathroom to wash my face to try to wake up. You kept screaming for me, desperate to get off the crib.

"I'm coming, *Pavito*," I said while I was still in the bathroom.

Suddenly, I heard a loud boom. My heart stopped. When I came out, you were on the floor. You had taken a fall of about four and a half feet. You were crying so hard. I ran to lift you up and I noticed the rail on your crib was not fully closed. I pressed the emergency button.

"I'm sorry, I'm sorry, I'm sorry," I kept saying.

A nurse came in and I explained what had happened. After she informed the doctor, they ordered some x-rays and other tests.

While they were getting your x-rays I could not stop crying and beating myself up for not locking the crib. I did not know if I should call your dad and ask him to come, or just hang on and wait. You are in a delicate state, your platelets are low. Platelets are those tiny soldiers that make your wounds heal. Any slip-up could be fatal.

I had nothing else to do but wait. When we went back to your room, you had calmed down but I was still upset. I don't really know if I was crying because of the scare or because of everything that was going on. I started to give you a bath and I know you don't like that because we do it on your crib with wet wipes. Even though I warm them up, you still get cold.

"Everything is alright, mom, everything is okay," you were saying even after what just had happened.

I am moved by how you notice that I am not okay. I try not to worry you, but when I am on my own, it is impossible to do it all.

Thank goodness everything was perfect when your tests came back. I don't know how, but it was as if nothing had happened. Not even a bump. God protected you, of that I am sure.

I called your dad to tell him everything while you were napping. I told him I could not take it anymore. It was impossible to be on top of everything. We had been living in hospitals for many months now and I needed some extra help that would give me a break during the nights. With the help of your godparents and an aunt from Tampico, Mexico, we found a special someone to watch over you and light up your nights. We will always be grateful for her light, which is fitting, because her name, Luz, means light in Spanish.

We agreed she would get here when you were already asleep, and I would come back before you woke up. At first, I had remorse. Now, I can really appreciate it. Like your dad said, "Nayeli, it could be years of living like this, no one can take it."

He was right, as usual. Thanks to that help, I am now more active, in a better mood, and with the same desire to live you have.

I would like to tell you about what I do when I am not with you.

I leave the hospital between 8:30 and 9 p.m. and go straight to the grocery store. I get to the apartment at around 10:30 p.m., put everything away and start cooking. Hospital food is horrible and unhealthy. Since you were a baby I have given you organic food. I have done some research and there are certain foods that help fight cancer cells. So, every week I make a meal plan for you that includes juices, almond milk, coconut water, chicken soup with ginger, and kale. I puree all your food, that is how you like it.

I have learned a million tricks to make you eat healthy foods.

I managed to sneak in an electric skittle and a mini fridge into your hospital room. I am so thankful for the nurses that pretend they don't notice the mini fridge covered by a bed sheet pretending to be a side table, because I usually eat the leftovers since I have no energy to fix something for myself.

While the food is cooling down, I do a load of laundry and take a hot shower. After five months of cold showers at the hospital, hot water is quite a blessing! When I get off the shower, I place the food in containers and put it in the fridge. I transfer the clothes to the dryer, then, I call your dad. I write for a little bit and then fold the laundry. I go to bed between 12:30 and 1 a.m. My body unplugs completely until 7 a.m. when my alarm goes off. Time to go back to reality. Between 7:30 and 8 a.m. I am back in the hospital, ready to make you happy.

Sometimes I feel as if I haven't seen you in weeks. It makes me happy to see you wake up with a big smile on your face. I am so used to being with you all day.

I love you with all my heart. And, how does my heart beat for you?

After many months of not going out beyond the hallway, you got permission to go to the courtyard. Your "field trip" happened to be when my aunt from Tampico was here helping us. At first, you held onto me confused. You did not understand what was happening. You were scared. But then, you ran towards the flowers. It was wrong of me, but I let you touch the soil, leaves, and plants. I was making sure you did not touch your face, and I would wash your hands often. You were always an outdoorsy kid. You were so happy, and so was I. Seeing you this happy made everything worth it. It was a great day for both of us, just thinking of it makes my eyes misty… I wish every day could be like that!

You were doing so well that they gave us some wonderful news. We had permission to leave the hospital for a week! Can you imagine? After five months! I was ecstatic!

I started taking some of your toys to the apartment. I checked for places I could take you where there would not be a lot of people. I made a lot of plans, I was thrilled and excited. I finally called your dad and grandma with some good news:

"We get to be normal for a week!" I told them.

A day before leaving, you had a high fever. You were shaking. Remorse took over me. I started wondering if letting you enjoy the outdoors was the cause of this. Do I need to be like a strict soldier with a two-year-old boy that only wants to enjoy the world? I am hopeless not knowing how to care for you. I was so looking forward to go out and now, that is not going to happen.

They gave you antibiotics and it only made it worse. Luz was staying with you that night. I left the hospital and went straight home, I was exhausted. At 3 a.m. my phone rang.

"Your son is very sick, we need your permission to take him to the Intensive Care Unit if necessary," a doctor told me.

"Yes," I replied groggily, I even think I said it in Spanish.

Panicked, I took the car keys and ran to the parking lot in my pajamas and slippers. I had a hard time opening the car, my hands were shaking and I dropped the keys three times. I was bawling while driving to the hospital and I could see the big red numbers in the car's clock, it was 3:10 a.m.

"Jesus, I trust in You," I kept saying out loud.

This was the first and only time I got to the hospital in five minutes instead of 15. There were no cars on the road but I was also driving as fast as I could. It was 3:16 and I had already parked the car. Those six minutes seemed like hours.

As I was walking towards your room, I saw all the nurses looking at me with a look of "poor woman, we're so sorry." My heart started beating and I felt my legs go numb, I did not know what to expect. I took a deep breath and entered the room where ten doctors were surrounding your crib.

"What happened?" I asked.

"For a moment he stopped breathing, we're worried about his blood pressure, it's too low," one of them said.

Your skin looked purple and you had a rash all over your body. I quickly ran and hugged you. They started asking me all these questions that I could not answer. I was in shock. I wanted to get in a time machine and go back to those days when you cried at night because you were hungry and not because this horrible disease is taking over you. I felt absolutely helpless, small and alone, holding in my arms someone even smaller that completely depends on me.

Turns out you had an allergic reaction to one of the medicines. On top of that, you had a bacteria that infected your central line, which is the catheter where they pump the medicine to your heart, so they had to take it out and put a new catheter in your arm. We now have to wait until we get rid of the bacteria in order to go to surgery and restore the central line, because the veins in your arm are not going to be able to handle all that medicine.

I stayed up watching you sleep. I prayed and I cried. "Luis Pablo, you are so strong, you have to fight to get better, I admire your resilience, and your ability to adapt is amazing," I would tell you over and over again.

Luz was there with us, I asked her not to get scared, this was not an everyday thing and I really needed her.

Thank God it is Sunday already. A new week starts tomorrow and that is how I live my life now, one day at a time. Just like with this horrible disease, one day you are perfectly fine and the next one you are critically ill. Please remember that I love you with all my heart and I only want you to be happy. Please forgive me if I did something to cause this, my heart aches and I feel like the worst mother in the world. I want to make your days better and today, I have failed.

Yesterday, after getting no sleep at all, Luz came back so that I could get some rest. I was drained. I don't even know how I got to the car, I can only remember thinking about laying in bed like any other person without any problems and being able to sleep for hours. But I needed to stop at the store to get your coconut water. That was when I heard a siren and a voice telling me to pull over.

A police officer came to my window and asked for my driver's license because I had run a red light. As I handed it to her, I remembered that I had been in the United States for three months already, and if anything happened they could easily send me back to Mexico. I have had such a bad day that the simple thought of getting a ticket, with all the high expenses we have right now, made me cry.

"What's going on?" The officer asked in an angry and confused manner.

"It's my son, he has leukemia and yesterday they almost took him to ICU. I was just going to buy some things he needs and I can't believe I'm so distracted that I ran a red light. I have enough with what's going on at the hospital," I told her while wiping away my tears.

Her facial expression started to change. She tore up the papers and gave me my driver's license back.

"Go home and get some rest, you look really tired. Please, don't drive like this, your son could lose his mother while he's in the hospital," she told me.

"Thank you so much! I promise you this won't happen again."

It was a small miracle that the officer let me go, but she told me something very disturbing on an already difficult day. I could not sleep thinking about what would happen if something happens to me while you are in the hospital. I started to worry about people I have never worried before: immigrants. How can they live with the fear of being deported? All those people fighting for a dream. I wonder if someday we will understand that more than nationalities, we have feelings. We are all human beings and it would be nice if we start treating each other like such.

I called your dad to tell him everything that happened today. He will fly to Houston tomorrow to be with us. Even if we are apart, my admiration and love for him grow each day.

I love you, Luis Pablo. And, how does my heart beat for you?

Nayeli Pereznegrón
March 17, 2014

I have learned that I can't change a diagnosis, but I can change the attitude I have towards it. We should be taught to smile a little more during sad times, that way things would be easier. I've seen constantly depressed moms with constantly depressed children. Nobody would ever choose this road, but we can definitely choose to make it as manageable as possible. When you focus on the good in each day, the journey becomes less daunting for mother and child. #happykids #happymoms #attitude #lpap #stpatricksday #herointraining #fighter #futureamlsurvivor

👍 122   💬 14   ➤ 1

At last, some good news! You started to get better! Therefore, after half a year in isolation, we were allowed to go home for five days. Your doctors had some conditions, though. For example, I have to be your nurse, that is why I had to learn how to clean your catheter and administer medicine through your central line. I wrote down a schedule of all the drugs you have to take on a big board on the wall. You will have me as your personal nurse at home, 24 hours a day. The idea of doing something wrong makes me nervous, but I know together we'll be able to do this, after all, your dad has learned how to do it, too. I am so proud of myself for overcoming my fears, you lead me by example every day when you overcome yours. You are my great little teacher, sometimes I feel like you are the one doing the parenting.

Luis Pablo and his family in the apartment.

Luis Pablo enjoying life out of the hospital.

I am so happy I get to spend these days with you that I am not going to write. I only want to enjoy being with you, plus I don't think I could ever put into words all the happiness I am feeling right now. This break will be so good for all of us.

We are back in the hospital. Being in the apartment was wonderful and a bit tiring. You were very happy, laughed a lot, and acted mischievous like any other kid. You let yourself loose and started walking again on your own. We enjoyed ourselves like a normal family. Your auntie Ale's visit was a nice surprise, she chose to be with us as her graduation gift. We now have a doctor at home, I am so proud of her and I know someday you will too.

Your first chemo round went perfectly, that means we will continue with the treatment and there is no need for a transplant for now. I am so grateful to God. The compatibility tests showed dad is not a match, and I am a 50% match. If you ever need a transplant I could be an option. I would be glad and happy to give you my heart if you needed it.

I have grown close to the nurses and especially to your oncologist, Dr. Dreyer. She gave me her cell phone number, something that rarely happens in this country. Having her number gives me peace of mind. At least I know I can contact her if there is ever any trouble. She said she has never met such a strong child, and she is impressed by how well you did on your chemo. You are amazing my love, I don't say this as your mom, I say it as a person who admires you and learns from you every day. You are my great little teacher, thank you for teaching me so many things. Of course I had to be strong if the Hulk is my very own child! My heart will never stop beating for you and because of you.

We have had some long days at the hospital and I have barely written, I spend most of my time on you. We have learned to enjoy each other, we laugh non-stop, we go for strolls and try to be happy in this world full of love that we have built in this hospital of which I am now fond of.

We have bad cell phone reception in your room. If I want to text someone to check in on them or to share some news, I wait until you're asleep and go to the lobby where the signal is better. That is when I have 30 minutes to catch up with everybody.

You still hate your baths. It was never easy, but now it has become a daily battle. Whenever grandma is here, I ask her to do it for me because I cannot bear it. My heart aches every time you make that pain face as we lift your arms up while I pass a wet wipe. I notice how damaged your skin is and how it sticks to your bones. I notice how skinny you are, all the bruises you have, and the

Luis Pablo's oncologist ZoAnn Dreyer

scars from all the needles. That is why I avoid doing it if I can. We have been in the hospital for six months now. I cannot even begin to tell you how everything that we have been through is far from a stroll in the park, but I have to recognize that I have learned to focus on the good, I have no other choice. Life has taught me this, and in spite of everything, things are not that bad. We are together and we have learned to connect, just by looking at you I can tell when you are about to get sick, when you are going to be hungry, or the face you will make when you find out what you will have for dinner. We have a natural connection simply because I am your mother, but it has become stronger with all the things we have been through. I have also learned a little bit about medicine. Now, I know which drugs make you grouchy and which ones have no side effects on you. I know the medicines you are supposed to get before each transfusion, and the ones you are supposed to have with food. I can perfectly read your lab results now, I know how your platelet count is doing, I can tell when you are going to need a transfusion or when something is not looking good. It is as if we are the same person, I breathe through you, for you, and because of you.

Today is a day to remember. Doctors and nurses came and filled your room with toys as an "award" for being so courageous. You deserve it for being so brave and well-behaved. They are in awe of you because you make no fuss when they draw blood or clean your catheter. I try to cheer for you every time after they poke you with a needle, and when I forget to do so, you remind me and ask for your chant. You are a fighter, you are making a mark in my life and in the lives of many others. You were so excited with all your gifts that you fell asleep very fast.

Nayeli Pereznegrón
April 21, 2014

Good evening.

When you're going through unusual situations where the person next door is suffering, the one across the hall is fighting for their life, and mothers and their sick children come into this hospital daily, you realize how transient life can be. Your shift changes, you start to see with your heart instead of your eyes. When I know someone is suffering, it hurts me, much more so when it's someone I care about. My heart and my prayers are especially with the people of Saltillo who are suffering after some bad news this Holy Week. God is good and we can always find strength in Him. Keep the faith!

Back at the hospital, children were discharged and new families arrived. My heart shrinks whenever I see new people coming in. It's always the same face, the same look of concern, I want to tell them that everything passes, that you get used to it, and that you learn to be happy in here. I look at them and I remember when they first told me that my son not only had leukemia, but he had the rarest and worst of them all, "it's like winning the lottery twice" (words that I'm never going to forget), I never thought I would be this calm. You get used to this hospital and you even grow fond of it! LPAP finished his second round of chemo yesterday, two per day, sometimes even three. He did great! I'm so proud of him and I admire him so much. He had no nausea, no loss of appetite, he gained weight and is super happy. Please pray so that now that he's in neutropenic state (he has ZERO antibodies) he doesn't catch anything and that his numbers go up faster than last time.

It was a nice emotional week, I think it was the best one since we started this journey. The three of us got to be together as a family again, and people we love were there with us too.

👍 2 mil   💬 165   ➢ 2

It is official! The last round, and if everything goes well, we will be out of here! This is the most important and intense stage of your treatment. Your heart has been through so much and it is tired. These will be the most difficult chemotherapies as well as the worst of fevers, infections, and blisters. This time, it will be a different drug, a very aggressive one.

This last stage can unleash many things, that is why we will be praying constantly for you to withstand this.

It will be two months before we are done and find out if we have beat cancer. If so, we will go back home but we will have to come back for monthly check-ups for two years, since we are dealing with a very aggressive form of leukemia. The chances of it coming back are very high. If it doesn't work out, our next option would be a transplant.

No more chemo!

When we were transferred to the 9th floor, oncology, I saw a big sign on one of the rooms "Congratulations on your last chemo!" I never thought I would see this day, but today that same sign is hanging from your door.

My spirits have lifted. I cannot believe we have come this far. The light at the end of the tunnel is finally starting to show up. I admire you so much, son! And, how does my heart beat for you?

Nayeli Pereznegrón
May 12, 2014

About to start the procedure for his first chemo of the third round.

I've learned to live for today, I don't know if that's the best thing to do but I find it less stressful. I can't be thinking about the things that could be, because many times I just worry and our attitude affect us. Every person and every situation is different.

Today I learned this round will be 10 times stronger than the last ones, the dosage will be 10 times more. I'm asking you for 10 times the prayers so that my little one maintains his good spirits.

This round will be shorter: 15 days for the first block, eight for the second, and five days for the last one, with three daily chemo sessions (15 total). Doctors believe his immune system will endure more damage than the previous times, but they've said that since the beginning and honestly, we're doing great.

With the help of God, we'll be okay this time too. As always, thank you for your love and support! Here we go, let's give this third round everything we've got! 10 times stronger!

👍 1.5 mil   💬 371   ➤ 32

Nayeli Pereznegrón
June 18, 2014

It's official! Today you had the last chemo of your treatment, they can't give you more. You had 92 chemo sessions in total, including 38 on this third round. We trust that God will help us conquer this and we won't need more treatment. We are so happy to be done! You had no fever, and even with the stronger dose, it seemed like they weren't even doing anything to you, I'm not lying! Now your immune system will start to slow down and we'll hit zero soon, I'm hoping no bug will bother you and ruin your discharge from the hospital. One more month until we find out if the treatment worked. My beloved #superherointraining is about to graduate. You completed the courses today, we're just waiting on the final exam to get your official superhero degree. Tomorrow will be a long day, we'll finally find out if the chemo worked. Although we won't be hearing any news tomorrow, it is an important day for you, baby. We have faith that the miracle is already done, but still, I can't help but feel a knot in my stomach while you're laying here sleeping next to me.

👍 5.6 mil   💬 371   ➤ 32

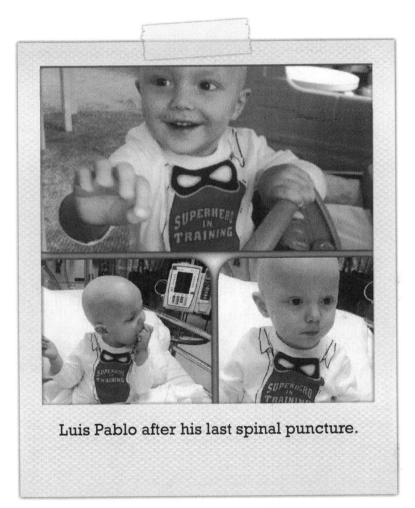

Luis Pablo after his last spinal puncture.

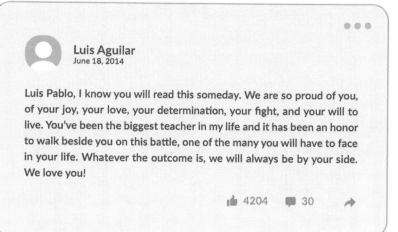

Al last, the news we have been longing for, the news we prayed for and the one I begged God to hear. I cannot contain my excitement! We beat cancer!

We could not believe it! Our dear oncologist, Dr. ZoAnn Dreyer, could not believe it either. The minute she had the results, she texted us saying we could pack our bags and go back to our dear Mexico. After eight months away, we will go back to our home, to our world. My heart could burst with happiness. You are happy too, you understand perfectly that this is over and that we will play outside again.

I get excited just thinking that one day we will take you to meet Mickey Mouse! You love him so much! I don't know how to thank God and all the people that prayed for you, as well as the ones who donated blood and platelets. This victory is God's work and the work of all the people that joined your battle in different ways. You must remember this miracle forever, and never forget that you have a duty to help others, even if you don't know them.

I am deeply grateful for the staff at this hospital. I have to confess I am a little sad knowing that we will not see them again. We are leaving tomorrow, so I have learned by heart the smell of the hospital, I have traced your bald head on my cheek, I have hugged the sofa-bed and as I felt the cold purple plastic, I squeezed it as hard as I could. I am hugging everything that for a moment represented something bad, because I don't want to forget anything. I know that remembering this will make me a better person, I will never complain about tomorrow, today is a big day in our history.

Tomorrow we will be free again. We will feel the sunlight, the breeze, the rain, Houston's fresh air. So many feelings! You are beginning a new story with your parents, and I am sure everything will be better than ever, because of all the things we have seen and learned in this hospital. I could not be more proud of you. Thank you for being my biggest teacher all this time, and for always bringing out the best of you. I will forever be in debt to you for pushing me to be a better person. Tomorrow is the beginning of a long and happy life together.

Luis Pablo watching the cars go by like every afternoon.

Hello, Luis Pablo,

We have been so happy with you in the apartment. We have been enjoying the outdoors and the beautiful parks in this city. Yesterday, we came back from Galveston. We went there for two days to escape. Even though you still cannot get in the ocean, you were so happy playing in the sand. You enjoyed the water, rocks, and starfish. You were running around constantly saying "Wow!" You were amazed by every thing that crossed your path. I keep thanking God for allowing me to see you get well.

We already started packing, we will soon go back to our home in Saltillo. Finally, after all this time. I am happy to go back home!

Cancer free!

BACK HOME

Today, we finally woke up as a family. The first night being apart was not easy. You had a hard time falling asleep and I had to go to your room several times during the night to soothe you and help you fall back asleep. For eight months we went to bed and woke up together, now we have to get used to this.

You still need a lot of care. You need to be in a sanitized environment, that is why I have been making sure your areas are squeaky-clean. We were out of the house for a long time and now there is dust everywhere.

Somebody once told me life was going to split before and after cancer. So true! Although all things have worked out, you still haven't managed to adjust. In your eyes, the house is so big compared to that tiny hospital room we made our home. I am sure you miss it because I cannot leave your side even for a second. There has been a lot of changes, but I know this is all part of the process and I thank God I get to experience this.

My Facebook account is overflowing with messages from people that have cancer or that know somebody that has cancer. I haven't been able to read them all. I feel bad but I am very careful with the time I have, I don't want to spend it reading my emails or on the phone with my friends, I would rather enjoy my time with you and your dad. Besides, after such a long confinement, I don't feel comfortable going out.

I know the fact that we are home would not have been possible without God's will and the help of so many people. This is a shared victory.

Luis Pablo, we must never forget to be thankful for this miracle. We are in debt with so many people. Your father and I have been thinking about helping other children with cancer and we already told you about this project. We have started to make some sketches for a logo with angel wings, because there is nothing that better describes all those children that are fighting this horrible disease. You only smile at every update and draft that we show you.

Someday, we will help many kids, you will see. It is only a matter of time and of you getting better. I vow to do this in appreciation for all the support we had. I hope you do this too, and that you do it from the heart, like we do. Remember that in this life, the best thing we can do is to show our gratitude with actions, because words are just dust in the wind. A coherent person always thinks, talks, and acts with their ideals in their heart and putting their values before everything.

We attended a wedding this past weekend. I could not help but cry when the groom entered the church with his mom by his side. "Many times I've asked God to let me walk Luis Pablo down the aisle," I told your dad.

I started doing that during your treatment. Maybe it is a silly dream, I don't even know if you will want to get married one day. But today, I long for that moment and I am sure God will make it happen. And when it happens, we will read this together and we will feel so close to God just like we did when we were in the hospital.

It has been a week since I have written. I am just enjoying our life here and every single thing we do together. But, you had a nosebleed yesterday and just the thought of you not having enough platelets sent shivers down my spine. You look pale and have dark circles under your eyes. Everyone in the family tells me it is all in my mind. I don't know, it could be, but will I have to live with this fear for the rest of my life?

I don't know if I could take it if this horrible disease ever comes back, I don't think I could withstand watching you go through that again. Having these thoughts upsets me, but my heart feels restless. I am worried about you.

Today, you woke up with a fever and I immediately called your dad in tears to tell him the cancer was back.

Ready to have my scans and biopsies done!

"How do you know? Did you go to the doctor already?" he replied enraged.

I told him we were headed over there but that my heart could tell. He tried to reassure me you were fine by saying that since your immune system was still weak, there was a high possibility that a virus could be the culprit. He asked me to calm down, but there was no way of doing that. My heart, my mind, and my soul could sense it.

When we got to the hospital, our dear pediatrician ordered some test to put me at ease. He also believed it could be a virus, but the results showed a high number of lactate dehydrogenase. The high levels of this enzyme was the reason we took you to the hospital in Monterrey the first time.

He told me not to worry, he said it could be something else, but right away, I let Dr. Dreyer know. She suggested we bring you back to Houston to do a marrow puncture and find out for sure what was going on.

Marcelo, your pediatrician, quickly arranged a platelet transfusion just to be safe. A childhood friend of mine offered to be your donor, she even stayed with you at the hospital while your dad got the plane tickets and I packed our bags and made arrangements.

I was going back to the nightmare I thought was over. Fear took over me and the only thing I could say was: "God, please give me strength because I used it all on the first stage of this illness." This time is different, we will face a stronger cancer in a weakened body, I know what to expect, I know what we will see, I saw it in other patients, I am so scared.

We were only in our house for three weeks. I will update you whenever I can.

RELAPSE

My dearest boy,

It has been three weeks since the diagnosis was confirmed. Your cancer is back and it is more aggressive than before. The studies showed metastasis and cancerous cells in your little head. I have to confess, I have cried more now than when we first found out about your illness. It breaks my heart to see you suffer again..

They say relapses are far worse in every way, including the emotional aspect. My first wound was not completely healed and now I am getting another cut in the same place. We only got to be in our home for three weeks. Every day I would thank God for your life and for my own, for the chance of waking up and hear you sing in your crib waiting for me to pick you up. You greeted me each morning with the biggest smile and a bear hug, you would eat your breakfast and then we would head out to the backyard to explore. We were so happy to get to enjoy life again.

Our option right now is a bone marrow transplant, my greatest fear is now a reality. I have to process this news as quickly as possible so that we can tackle this problem with the best attitude that I can.

Your grandparents are here already. They cut short their 30th wedding anniversary trip to be with us. As always, they are helping to take care of you. I could not do it on my own, my body was experiencing an extreme exhaustion and dad was dealing with all the arrangements needed for us to face this.

We rented a bigger apartment this time. Doctors are saying that after the transplant, you will have to stay in the hospital for a hundred days, and then go to the hospital daily. We have a long road ahead of us, but I will always be right by your side. I am not going to rest until you are healthy and we take you back to Mexico.

Your father will be making an even bigger effort this time. He decided he will work two weeks in Saltillo, and then spend two weeks with us. From the bottom of my heart, I wish him well in his projects. I ask God to always bless him, he is a great man! I admire him deeply. I feel very lucky and I am so grateful that he is the one by our side fighting this battle.

When everybody went back to Saltillo, your godmother Ale, who recently graduated from medical school, came to the rescue. We made a schedule to make things easier. I am with you during the mornings while your aunt goes to the gym and studies for her residency exams. In the afternoons, I go to yoga class. I need to do something to keep my mind off things and to force my body to move. I am also trying to strengthen my physical and emotional well-being before facing the most difficult stage yet: the transplant. Every day at yoga class, I give it all for youand for your health.

We have had some hard and complicated days. Your body is hosting a bacteria. You have lost so much weight, and no matter what I do, I cannot get you to eat. You look tired and you don't understand what is happening. You keep asking for dad, you miss him so much.

We still haven't met the doctor in charge of your transplant. We have a lot of questions, and we have been trying to speak to her for two weeks with no luck. I trust God and your oncologist, who says she is the best option for you. Also, we still haven't found a bone marrow donor, but I try to remember what you say all the time: Everything will be all right. Remember that I love you with all my heart, my darling boy.

Nayeli Pereznegrón
September 27, 2014

Today marks one month since we came back to the hospital scene and to this new world of transplants. We were admitted to the hospital on August 27, which happened to be on the same date of the first time you were admitted here first, January 27. Just over a month ago, we thought our life was perfect, with a healthy child. My husband and I went to a wedding and we really enjoyed it. After such a long time of only seeing each other some weekends, and with so many worries and concerns, we understood we had the chance to be happy and to seize every moment.

We feel special for having spent that month out of the hospital, for having enjoyed that time knowing that everything was fine, and cherishing every single day we spent at home. That was a small break that God gave us in the midst of this long road we have ahead before the full and complete recovery of our son. Today is Luis Pablo's day number 15 without a working immune system. Before, it would only take him 7 to 10 days to start producing antibodies. Every day that goes by like this is a torment, but we're hoping he soon starts to get well and we won't have any more scares.

He asks for his dad and grandpa all the time. I think he is sick of being around women all the time, haha! Because all of his doctors and nurses are women too! A few weeks ago, he Skyped with his dad and he recognized our house, he asked to see his crib, he would keep saying "Yes, yes, yes," and "outside." My husband went out and showed him our yard, he started crying and kept saying "yes, yes!" His hair started to fall off again, that's the least of our worries, but he just looks to handsome with those brows and eyelashes —they represented a miracle for us for a few months there. Still, no news on the donor. But that just means they're doing a very meticulous job finding the one who will save my boy. On Monday they'll do a scan on his head to see if the cancer cells he had are now gone after this last chemo. Please pray for him!

👍 1.8 mil 💬 200 ➤ 19

What a month!

I have less and less time to write each day. I'm always exhausted, although sometimes I don't write simply because I don't want to share any more bad news with you.

You are not in remission. We have tried every chemotherapy available and the cancer is still there. This complicates everything, because in order for you to get a bone marrow transplant, there must be no cancerous cells in your body. Plus, we still have no donor.

I'm writing from the Intensive Care floor.

Yesterday, our day began just like any other, with me begging you to have some breakfast. It has been months since you've had a full meal, you keep spitting your food saying it tastes like the magnets on the fridge. Sometimes, you have a bite here and there just to make me happy, but you are never really hungry.

All of a sudden, we noticed a putrefied smell that had taken over the room. The smell was so strong that your dad, grandma, and me started joking about who would be the brave one to change your diaper. I started to feel sick just from the smell, your skin was quite yellow, but you were laughing and started gagging too, you thought it was funny to make the noise without actually being nauseous.

Your grandma volunteered to change your diaper. The moment she unfolded it, I was shocked to see it filled with blood. It was so much blood that within seconds your crib sheets were covered in blood too. I ran for the emergency call button, three nurses came in.

"Now we know where that reek was coming from," one of them said as she covered her nose.

I guess the smell had reached the hallway. The second nurse took a step back when she saw the blood, and the third one ran to get the doctor on call, who called more doctors. Suddenly, our room was filled with people in white coats. Once again, we found ourselves in a critical situation. The doctors were saying things I couldn't understand, the only thing I heard was "We have to act now or we're going to lose him." I felt numb.

The doctors started to roll your bed. Dad and I stood by your side, we ran down the hospital hallways with the doctors. You were surrounded by stressed faces and we did not want you to be scared so we started singing. You had no idea what was happening, but you started to sing too and you gave us the weakest smile I have ever seen as blood kept running down the bed.

Right there, one of the nurses put his hand on my shoulder.

"He is amazing," he said.

I kept singing to keep you distracted. At the same time, tears were running down my face.

We were in the ICU for the first time. The first thing I saw was a child with cancer on a ventilator. I shuddered and I begged God to protect you. The doctors stopped at the drapes before entering a room and asked us to wait there.

"What? But he's my son!" I said.

"Yes ma'am, but we must act fast and you can't be inside, there's too many people there, help us by not getting in the way."

"Okay then, but let us give him our blessing."

They let us in, I gave you a kiss with all of my love and I saw even more blood everywhere. That was the first time I thought I might not see you again. I hugged you and told you to remember that no matter what you saw or heard, mom and dad would be waiting for you outside and that we would never stop waiting for you. Weakened by the loss of blood, you managed to nod.

Outside, your dad hugged me tightly. While we were walking towards the waiting area, I fell to the floor and I cried with all my might, your dad did too. After a few minutes, he hugged me and said: "We'll get through this, we have to be strong for him."

Your grandparents witnessed everything from the ICU waiting

74

room. I could tell they had been crying too, but with a calm voice they asked how you were doing.

"I don't know," I replied sharply wishing they wouldn't start asking me questions, and they didn't.

Your grandpa sat next to me and grabbed my hand tightly.

"Oh Sweetheart! I would give my life to make all of this go away," he told me after giving me a kiss.

His eyes were filled with tears, but my eyes were dry. I could only stare at the door where they took you, waiting for somebody to come out with some news.

It was almost nighttime and we still knew nothing about you. Your dad and I decided to reach out to a fellow Hispanic and member of the ICU group of doctors, Dr. George, who is now like a member of our family. It was his day off but he quickly came to the hospital. When he saw your dad sleeping on the floor, he suggested we look for a spot at the Ronald McDonald's house, right across from the ICU.

Luis Pablo and Dr. George.

Luis Pablo, your father and I have learned to accept all the help we are offered, because we never know when we will get it again. Dr. George got us a room there, we agreed that my sister Ale and Luz would stay and wait for an update and that your grandparents would go back to the hotel.

We went to our room at the Ronald McDonald's house. It was amazing. I never imagined there could be a place like that in a hospital. It had clean sheets and hot water. Your dad took a shower and I fell asleep. I woke up at 7 a.m., your dad was still asleep, I got ready and went out running to see what had happened. Luz and Ale were sleeping on some blue chairs they had arranged to lay on.

Over two thousand people in social media together for Luis Pablo.

I went to the desk to ask how you were doing, but there were still no news. I called "your uncle" George, and he told me you had lost a lot of blood and the doctors were still trying to stabilize you, so we were not allowed to see you yet.

After I learned about your condition, I went to get some coffee and I took a moment to write on your Facebook group. I let everybody know that you were critically ill and with all my heart I asked them to please pray for you. In less than ten minutes, all the profile pictures started to change to a picture of you that said *#recemosporLuisPablo* (Pray for Luis Pablo.) Again, I was amazed by the power of social media and the love of friends and strangers.

We were all sitting in the waiting room, staring at nothing and concentrated in our own thoughts. A doctor finally came out asking for Luis Pablo's family, we all stood up but she only wanted to speak to the parents.

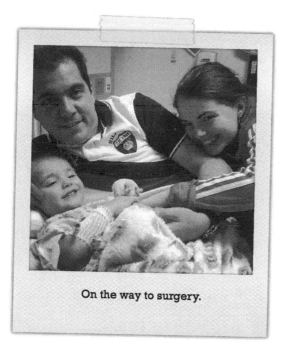

On the way to surgery.

Dad and I entered the ICU. There, the doctor told us sometimes things happen without a medical explanation, like what had happened to you yesterday. The lab results and x-rays showed nothing, the only thing they knew was that you had lost a lot of blood. But suddenly, everything was back to normal and they did not know for sure what had caused this.

"But, how will you be sure this won't happen again if you have no idea what it is?" I asked them.

"No, we can't be sure, because like you said, we don't know what caused it. Again, sometimes things don't have an explanation. The important thing is that Luis Pablo is now stable and you can see him," she said.

We ran towards your bed and I noticed you were extremely calm, looking at the light on the ceiling, as if you were trying to figure something out. You were so focused that you didn't even notice we were there.

"Luis Pablo," your dad said.

A smile lit up your face and you turned to see us. You asked for you iPad right away, you wanted to sing, and we did! But you only sang two songs, because you fell asleep. You were tired and weak.

We thought once you were stable they would take you back to your room, but the doctor asked to speak with us to tell us that a fungus had entered your body and had settled really close to your brain. They will have to perform an emergency surgery and scrape it in order to get rid of it. There are a lot of risks, but we have no other option. I will write you soon with better news, I promise. Remember that I love you.

By the way, it is my birthday today and my only wish is that you get well. And, how does my heart beat for you?

Nayeli Pereznegrón
October 14, 2014

We received some very bad news today... We've seen so many doctors that I don't even remember who was in each of the teams: gastro, respiratory, infectious diseases, oncology, hematology, cardio, surgical, and neurosurgery.

They discovered a fungal infection behind Luis Pablo's skull, on the brain. The team of neurosurgeons said there's nothing they can do about it, but our oncologist Dr. Dreyer had an idea. We were asked if we wanted to continue fighting or if we would rather bring our child home to enjoy "quality of life", where no one would see him, with risks of infections, and fungi, and fevers. We said that as long as there is a chance, we would fight with everything we've got. Turns out there is a chance, but he could also die -exact same words- however, our doctor is confident that this plan will work given that Luis Pablo is an incredibly strong child that never gives up and continues fighting. We were told they've done this before successfully, so we're continuing this battle.

The plan is to give him an ATOMIC BOMB of chemo, beginning this Friday, to try to get him in remission and go to transplant after that. He'll do that while the fungus is still there and it will be years before it's gone. We have to pray really hard for Luis Pablo to endure this, and for the cancer and fungus to be kept under control. Only those who have gone through a similar situation can understand. We won't give up, but knowing our limitations and trying to be as realistic as possible, two things are very clear to us:

1. This boy is an angel that God has given us on a loan to complete a mission, and once he completes it (even if we don't understand it) he will go back where he belongs. If that's so, from the bottom of my heart I can tell that we would go through all of this again in order to meet him and enjoy him for two years.

2. This boy will be a testament to a great miracle even after everything we've faced. Luis Pablo will pull through this and will help a lot of people.

Let's pray for God to grant us option number two. Today, I'm still writing as an inspiration and thinking that he will read this one day.

We are fully surrendered in God's arms and doing everything humanly possible to overcome this.

We've tried everything, his diet, teas, essential oils, and a lot of extra help that hasn't worked. Only God has the final say. We have the best doctors, we're definitely in the best hands.

We thank you all for your prayers, rosaries, good vibes, sacrifices, energy, and all things positive. We're asking more than ever that you continue to do so, everything helps.

Today has been a hard day, but even so, the sun will come out tomorrow and it will bring a new chance of living. We've made Luis Pablo incredibly happy, it shows, and we will keep on doing so! Our mission as parents is to make our kids happy for as long as God lets us, hopefully God will give us many more years together. Please, more than ever, let's pray for this to be true. We are counting on YOU! This wonderful team that's responsible for the only good news we've had this month. Thank you from the bottom of my heart!

WE ARE NOT AFRAID, GOD IS WITH US!

FUNGUS

You had a surgery today, and last week you had four. Doctors haven't been able to get rid of the fungus completely. It is lodged between the division of your nose and your brain, which makes it even more dangerous. Only God knows how many more surgeries you will have. You always come out of the OR with a lot of pain, this makes me suffer, but if I am completely honest, I don't think I would have been able to put up with this much. You are amazing!

The medicine they are giving you is not working, so they will do a white blood cell transfusion (granulocytes) that will help fight the fungus. This is an experimental treatment, there is no evidence that it works but they will try it on you. I really hope it works because all these complications are just bumps in the road that keep us from going to transplant. The doctors' main concern right now is to control the fungal infection, you haven't had any more chemotherapy and we are all afraid that with this leg up, the cancer could take over other parts of your body.

I literally wanted to die when I learned you needed about 30 donors to be able to start the treatment.

"Where are we going to find them?" I asked your dad.

"Leave it to God," he told me. "Don't take on burdens we can't afford to carry right now."

Not knowing if I should cry, laugh, or throw myself on the floor, I decided to put myself in God's hands. I went to the chapel at the hospital. It is like a space for meditation for every person regarding their religious views, so that they can have a peaceful moment and talk to their god. There is a little tree where you can put your petitions. There, without thinking I wrote this:

> God, I can't take it anymore. My heart, my mind, and my body can't stand this much. Please, from the core of my being, help me to carry through this. Take my son's illness, I can't bear it anymore, please just give me the strength I need and the ability to see things clearly. Give me whatever a mother needs in times like this, teach me how to fully trust you, fill my heart with love and comfort it, because right now it feels lonely and sad. I BEG YOU, I'm desperate.

After I finished writing, I hung the note from the tree and went back to you. The moment I posted on your Facebook page that you needed donors, over 250 people sent their information. God has been there every stage of your life, always remember that He has done a lot for you and don't forget to donate, to help others like others did for you.

I hope I am back with good news soon. I love you *Pavito*! I thank God for bringing you into my life, you are my everything, you are simply the best of me.

THANK YOU FOR MAKING ME A BETTER PERSON!

And, how does my heart beat for you?

The good news is that we have enough donors. It is an enormous effort, everything these people are doing, and I really appreciate it. First, they need to figure out if they are a match. To do that, they have to go to the hospital to do a blood transfusion. Once they find out they are a match, they get a call asking them if they are still interested in donating white blood cells and to explain the process in detail, some of them have withdrawn. After they accept to be your donor, the hospital sends some medicines to their house, as well as instructions on how to inject themselves on the leg. It is a small needle and it really doesn't hurt, I know because I already did it, but it just complicates the process. The steroids accelerate the production of white blood cells so that early the next day, they can donate them.

I am extremely moved by the people's response. I have to confess that if I was not going through this, I am not sure if I would ever volunteer as a donor. This is incredible, but do you want to know what the most amazing thing is? The proof of love that God has given me, it is what I asked Him on my note, and He is sending me all that through the people that have donated.

There are good people in the world, never doubt that, but they are doing good in silence. I wish more people would share the good things they are doing. I believe they could spread it to more and more people until a chain of good is formed and good deeds become trendy in a world where it seems like everything is fake.

People from many different backgrounds, ethnicities, and nationalities have given you life, from black, white, and Hispanics; to Catholics, Christians, Muslims, and atheists; married, divorced, or single, and people from the LGBTQ+ community as well. I have learned a big lesson, we all need everybody, without distinction, judgement, or scrutiny. In the end, love is what moves good people, and nothing more. Love is a universal religion, language, and movement. If we all decided to love more and judge less, the world would be a better place.

You are a living witness that good people exist in this world, you are so lucky to be carrying a part of them in you, cells from kind-hearted beings run in your blood.

When we are out of here we will have to help many more people to honor and commemorate all the good we have received. So many people have helped that it is hard to keep a list, but we show our gratitude by always praying for them.

My dearest big boy,

I cannot describe the amount of sorrow I'm feeling right now. Despite you getting donations of many "good soldiers" they still haven't been able to fight the fungus. I am extremely desperate thinking we are running out of options. My mind and my heart cannot come to terms with that. Plus, a doctor who is not on your team but that was on call when they detected the fungus, made me feel responsible for something that was nobody's fault. She had the nerve to tell me that the fungus probably came from the bottled coconut water that I give you. I was speechless, I didn't know what to say and guilt took over me.

Since we arrived at the hospital, I have been learning about healthy foods. I am always trying to feed you things that will boost and improve your immune system.

Your lab results always show low potassium, so I decided to start giving you semi-pasteurized coconut water, never straight from the fruit. Shortly after, your potassium levels were increasing. I was happy to know my research had paid off and that eating healthy foods was helping you. But today, my enthusiasm was destroyed. I am terrified to think that

I might have hurt you while trying to help you, or that I am in fact, the reason why that fungus is there. We will never know, but the doctor's attitude was deplorable. I hate that you won't be having any more coconut water, you like it so much and it is one of the few things that you have with no fuss. I know someday you will understand that everything we did was for your own good.

On the floor's medical team, there is a doctor that we have grown fond of. She checks on you daily, she says she is your girlfriend and you like to "flirt" with her. Today she told us, with a sad look on her face, that none of the treatments are working. The fungus keeps growing and is half a centimeter away from entering your brain. If it gets there, the damage would be fatal and beyond repair since there is no way to scrape the brain. On the other hand, the cancer keeps progressing.

The doctor spoke to us in English and I was surprised that you understood what she was saying. Silently, tears started running down my face as I listened. Right there, you began to get anxious like never before.

"Mom, mom, mom, mom," You kept saying in distress as she was talking.

After about five minutes, I turned to you.

"What it is, Luis Pablo?" I said, expecting you to ask for the iPad or a toy. But no, you needed my attention because I needed to hear you say:

"Jesus can heal, everything will be alright."

I was taken aback.

Your dad immediately said you were right, that everything was going to be okay and that we should trust Jesus. I was still speechless when the doctor asked what you had said. After I translated, tears came running down her cheeks.

"There's nothing I want more, my sweet Luis Pablo," she said as she stroked your head.

"Yes! Jesus can heal," you said with a smile.

It has been ten months since you were diagnosed and it still hurts me deeply every time they have to poke you to get a blood sample. I feel it in my heart, every surgery you have is a surgery in my heart, every fever weakens my soul.

During your relapse we have met the sad and cruel world you see in the movies and that you don't want to believe is true. A world different than the one we saw the first time you fought against cancer. It is true what they say, that you have to be more worried about a relapse than the diagnosis, now I understand that.

We keep getting bad news but our flame is still burning, we know your condition can change any minute, we already went through that. Cancer might spread all over you tiny body, but it won't touch our spirits or souls. We are fighting with a broken heart but our faith is indestructible.

You walk less and less each day. But there has been a lot of people that have run for you, they even sent you their medals. We have been knocked out several times during this battle, but these angels come and lift us up. Some other times we have gone silent after hearing some news, and the only prayers we can say are our tears, but people show up and pray for you.

Sometimes, your dad and I are broken into a million pieces, but then we see you smiling and for a moment, it feels like we are really protecting you. Some other days I am so worn out that I cannot even think of ways of entertaining you, and suddenly people we don't even know bring you toys to play with. There are times when I feel so lonely, but somebody always shows up to remind me that I am alive. And on the days that I forget to eat or whenever I am getting tired of hospital's salads, a volunteer shows up with a warm meal.

I know all this is because of God, because no matter what you are going through, if you surrender to his arms, He will send you everything you need. We are a very blessed family, that is why we are confident that we will soon get some good news.

We learned about your condition two days ago. Since then, I have been asking for prayers in every prayer group there is, especially in yours. Thousands of people are praying for you and on your behalf. After I posted, I started getting messages almost immediately about Masses being offered for you in 13 different cities: Houston, Laredo, McAllen, Saltillo, Monterrey, Acuña, Piedras Negras, León, Mexico City, Veracruz, Torreón, Querétaro, and Celaya.

I am so grateful for all the love, and although it seems like my heart seems to be beating with much less intensity these days, my heartbeat is still here, beating for you. I thank God, I thank you, and I thank all those people that are praying for us. There is no doubt in my heart that all those prayers are the reason we are still standing.

I love you.

I've received many messages. Whenever I have a chance, I read them and I find phrases like: I'm sorry, there are no words, I'm with you, I feel your pain.

I can't thank you enough for all your thoughtfulness during this journey we're living, but we're still standing! We're still in the battle! There is nothing to be sorry about, we just have a lot to be thankful for because this superhero is here with us. I would like to explain that even though we're hurt by the news, WE ARE NOT AFRAID... We are experiencing this unexplained peace, but we need to feel happiness again. Besides, my heart can feel that things will be okay, and if that's not the case, we are trying to be ready to cope with that, I say try because I would be lying if I told you that we're prepared for something no one is really prepared for.

Today we have a chance! A light! I thank God because there's still something to do. This is not over, and even when it ends, something else will begin, something that I'm sure is way better than we can imagine because our human mind is limited and it won't let us think beyond this earthly realm.

A dear friend of mine that has a great influence on me said: "Luis Pablo is ALREADY a miracle, for everything he's done, for the hearts he has touched, because he is always smiling, because he faces pain with a smile on his face." I've never noticed it. Life among doctors and hospitals is hectic and there's not time for reflections, I hadn't made time to realize that THE MIRACLE ALREADY HAPPENED, since Luis Pablo came to this world after a complicated delivery. From day one he's been a fighter, HE HAS A STRONG SPIRIT.

We witnessed another miracle today. Luis Pablo received white blood cells donated by family and friends, old and new. He's going to need more, but this process is so slow that sometimes, kids run out of time. Pavito already has the first portion inside him, fighting the fungus along the medication right before starting chemo again. We don't expect to beat it, because like I said before, it will take years to eliminate that fungus, but at least we can keep it dormant while we focus on getting rid of the cancer. THOSE WHITE BLOOD CELLS REPRESENT ALL THE PEOPLE THAT ARE FIGHTING THIS FIGHT WITH US. We thought he would be getting the transfusion after his chemotherapy but amazingly we were able to get him part of the army beforehand. THANK YOU FOR EVERYTHING, DON'T FORGET ABOUT HIM... EVERY LITTLE THING HELPS!

Luis Pablo, today I have witnessed a miracle that I hope I can pass on to you, so that the day you read this you are able to experience it as deeply and intensely as I did.

You have been getting white blood cells for a week and it seemed to be doing nothing. Early today, you had a procedure done. The doctors wanted to try something else to keep the fungus from entering your brain.

To their surprise, they didn't find anything. Just like that. Without explanation, speechless and perplexed. The surgeon asked me not to get my hopes up, they were going to do more tests because it was very strange. They did a ton of x-rays, they put you in the "time machine" and nothing! Like one of the doctors said: "It's as if it was never there."

The only thing we did differently this time, was having an army of people praying and attending Mass for you.

We immediately asked to speak to your oncologist, who was just as surprised as we were.

"I am so happy, it's amazing, there's no trace of it," she said.

"But, how? What happened?" I asked.

"See, I've been doing this for years and very few times I've seen results that have no explanation, some people call it miracles, I don't know what to call it. I'm just very happy that this happened because that means we can continue chemo. Luis Pablo's cancer has spread and we need to focus on this."

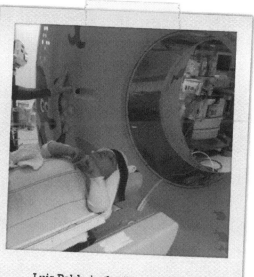

Luis Pablo in the "time machine."

Luis Pablo, I have no doubt that God can do anything and that He is with you. If the fungus had gotten to your brain, the pain would have been even worse than the one cancer makes you feel, and it would have defeated you in a horrible way.

God spoke to me today. I understood that He has a plan for each of us and I am not here to question that, but to fulfill it. I have put everything I have in his hands, including you. I know I have no control over anything and that I have been arrogant to think that I could change the course of his plans. Now, I know I have to be more grateful and ask less of Him. Luis Pablo, on the day you were first diagnosed, Marcelo your pediatrician said "Jesus, I trust in You," now I understand the meaning of those words. I fully trust Him, and accept his will.

I know I have to pray to be close to Him, because prayer connects us and it is a chance to thank Him for his many blessings, first and foremost for being alive. Before, I used to ask so many things of Him in my prayers. From now on, I will only say one thing: "Do unto me according to Your will and give me the strength I need to do so."

I don't need anything else, my son, my standpoint has changed. I felt God's presence deep in my heart and I was able to understand what others take years to do so. To fully put your trust in God is not to ask things from Him, it is thanking Him, and when something bad happens, something that really hurts, when you feel you cannot go on, don't ask Him for a miracle, you are a miracle already. Be grateful for his company and lean on Him.

Luis Pablo, I wish I could instill in you the power of prayer and the love of God, but words are not enough to explain it, you have to experience it in order to understand it. I feel lighter now that I have let go of things I know I cannot bear. I am going to devote myself to make you happy and to live happily every day. I am tired of being so worried all the time. From now on, I hope to be a less apprehensive mom. It is because of this miracle that I was able come up with this text that I wrote on your Facebook page. People seemed to like it, I think it touched some hearts and that makes me glad. I am happy to be able to share everything that God and you have taught me in this hospital.

Why did God send us this trial?

A mom at the hospital asked me this question when she learned my son did not enter remission and the cancer was spreading even further. I immediately blocked her words because I don't believe God "sends us" bad things.

That night, I kept thinking how could I explain this to a mother who daily sees the pain in her child with cancer, going through what she's going trough, begging God every single day to take this suffering, and in return she keeps getting more bad news. I realized it was pretty simple and I want to share it:

1. When the nurses told me that my son needed medicine and 32 injections to get a blood sample, and that one of those would be on his little head, I helped by holding him down.

2. When the doctors told me they would have to perform a surgery on my son to put a catheter, and that he would be in excruciating pain after the surgery, I gave him my blessing and left him in the hands of God and the surgeon.

3. When the doctors told me they had to scrape my child's nose to remove a fungus and that it was going to hurt, I held his legs to keep him from kicking while they did that.

4. When my son finally fell asleep after days of being in pain, and a nurse came in to check his pressure and his temperature, I didn't stop them.

5. When it took four people to restrain my son while they were doing yet another intravenous drip, I remember with his eyes he was asking me to do something to stop it, and even so I didn't.

6. When my son noticed the dolphins outside radiology and he started crying because he didn't want to go in the "time machine", I was the one who put him on the bed and helped the nurses tie up his arms. I could only see him crying from that astronaut suit I had to wear.

And I could keep on naming more examples.

I believe a two year old who knows nothing about life could complain that:

1. They poked me, they treated me badly and you did nothing to stop it.

2. Even though I cried because I didn't want to go with a stranger who did something weird to my forehead, you left me alone.

3. They did horrible things to my nose, I tried to fight them, I tried to escape, but you held my legs and prevented me from escaping pain.

4. You let them wake me up when I was so tired and wanted to sleep.

5. Four adults against a defenseless little boy like me, and you just stood there.

6. I asked not to be tied to that horrible bed, the "time machine", but you did it yourself and you even said "How fun!"

Everything we've done as Luis Pablo's parents has been for his own well-being. And even if at the time he didn't understand it and he wouldn't talk to me for hours, I know some day he will realize that everything we did was for his own good.

So? Are we acting like two-year-olds as we protest when God allow things we can't comprehend to happen?

Why is God allowing these things to happen to us?

Well that's easy! For the same reason that we as parents allow things to happen to our kids! They don't understand that everything we do is for their well-being. Then, we have to know that if God is making us go through certain experiences, He's only doing it because it is the best for us.

I'm not saying it doesn't hurt, I have an open wound ever since my eyes stopped seeing my healthy boy, but every day I use a balm named: Jesus I trust in You, and I can feel a relief and that inexplicable peace that God brings when we truly surrender in his arms and we trust his promises.

And from this viewpoint and feeling much stronger, I decided to watch The Heart of Christmas again, that movie I told you about. I gave you a bath, I gave you the massage you always ask for because your bones hurt, we prayed, and I laid next to you until you were asleep.

Then, I went to the couch, fixed my sheets, turned on my laptop and started watching. I couldn't help but cry, it made me relive everything we have been through. I found out the little boy in the movie had your same type of leukemia and that he is about your same age. After some treatment, he beats cancer and along with his parents, he goes back to his hometown, I didn't remember this part. Shortly after, the boy relapses. The cancer is back and they have to go back to the hospital and wait for a transplant.

As the story unfolds, a revolution of love and kindness is started, something similar to what you have accomplished. When I watched it the first time over a year ago, the story seemed distant, but now with your current state, everything seems more relatable. At the end of the movie, the boy passes away.

I grabbed the phone and called your father in tears. He was worried that I was calling because it was late and he was in Saltillo.

"What happened?" he asked.

"The movie! Luis, the movie!" I replied.

"What movie, Naye? I don't know what you're talking about."

"The movie we saw about the little boy with cancer. It is so real and so similar to what is happening to us. It's uncanny."

"Nayeli, please stop thinking that," Luis said. "There are a lot of differences, focus on those."

"No, Luis. I feel that God is talking to us through that movie. There's just so many coincidences: the diagnosis, the age, the firstborn, they moved to another city, the ICU, everything! Even the plush toy that he carried everywhere, just like Bebé, it had to be washed many times because the boy would throw up on him, and the parents ordered a replacement online. God is being very obvious!"

"Come on, Nayeli!" He answered upset.

I knew he was angry because he called me by my full name and he only does that when he is mad.

"Get those ideas off your head, please! Just be thankful and focus on the miracle that we've just witnessed on our son, that's God telling us that things will be different for Luis Pablo."

Luis Pablo with his blanket and Bebé that are with him everywhere he goes.

93

I understood he was right and I told him so, we said goodbye and hung up. My mind kept thinking about all the similarities and differences, but then I remembered that I had left everything in God's hands, so there was no need to worry. I closed my laptop and went to sleep.

Hi, *Pavo*,

You are turning two years old today! I never thought we would be celebrating in the hospital, but it was still a special day.

Everyone in your room was dressed up as Mickey Mouse, including you. We sang, played, blew the candles, and hit a piñata. Two other kids came to celebrate with us, you were so happy! Your doctor and nurses stopped by to say happy birthday and bring you gifts.

After that, we went to the family room and enjoyed a cake donated by Susan, a lovely volunteer who is always looking out for us. Some kids from the floor joined us, and Mickey Mouse stopped by too.

I was delighted! I felt so happy. I forgot that you are sick and enjoyed this day with you. I remembered the day you were born and everything we have experienced, and I reassured myself that I wouldn't change anything, not one single thing that we have been through because my prize, my blessing, my miracle, is you.

You received gifts literally from all over the world, you even got a teddy bear from Poland. I am so proud of you, maybe you don't understand what is going on, and that is why I will leave some

94

pictures of your gifts. Also, here are two posts, one from your dad who rarely posts, and one I wrote for you.

I love you, my baby. I'm sure that we will have many more birthdays to celebrate.

Messages from around the world for Luis Pablo.

Luis Aguilar
October 29 2014

Luis Pablo, you have no idea how glad I am to see you receive all this love. We thank God because the best gift that He has given us, is the chance to celebrate your birthday together as a family. My wish for you is that you become a prosperous happy man on anything you set out to do. And thank you for choosing us as your parents. You have taught us so much, we learn from you every day. You are amazing, son, I can't wait to see all the adventures we will have. I love you with all my heart. Your dad.

👍 4050   💬 125   ➤

Luis Pablo and his parents celebrating
his birthday in his hospital room.

Nayeli Pereznegrón
October 29, 2014 4

Dear son, today is your second birthday, and I'm celebrating two years of having the privilege of being a mom. You've spent half of your life in hospitals.

After almost 42 weeks of waiting, you decided to be born. Since then, you've been a warrior. We spent so many hours in labor that I got a fever, the moment the doctors stressed we had to go to the OR, I remember feeling overwhelmed. With fear and exhaustion I told your dad: "Put him first." That's when I discovered what a child means for a mother even before meeting them. Thank God we both made it out okay and the moment I saw your face and listened to you, I forgot everything. I met the miracle of life because of you. I was lucky enough to witness a second miracle when you beat cancer, and a third one when everything seemed lost because of a fungus that disappeared, and I'm about to witness a fourth miracle when you get your transplant. We are so blessed!

Always a special boy, a shining star, a child that was constantly approached by strangers at the supermarket to tell me about his special charm.

A year ago we were enjoying your first birthday party and the fever started that day, in fact, they had to give you a shot in order to control it.

Everything changed overnight... And these are some of the things that happened this past year. We stopped attending birthday parties and we started a real adventure.

- No more superheroes at birthday parties, you are meeting them in real life.

- We switched piñatas for an incredible robot that became your friend and has been attached to you all this time.

- Candy was replaced with medicine. You don't like either of them.

- I never took you to school, but you're learning things no school can teach. Lessons that not even I could have taught you, because I'm learning, too. We are lucky to go together to the school of life.

- I didn't post your first day of school pictures like I wanted to, but I did post a much happier picture on the first day you were out of the ICU.

- I don't have to worry about who your friends will be, because you are surrounded by angels. At such a young age you already know that not seeing a friend doesn't mean they're not with you, but that they're just holding you closer to God because they've earned a real pair of wings.

- I didn't write about how difficult it was to leave you with your teacher, but I always write about how hard it is to leave you with the surgeon. I imagine it's a similar feeling.

- I stopped following the milestones recommended for your age and I learned to praise you for every one of your individual successes. We celebrate every single thing you do, because to me, you've exceeded any expectations.

- No teacher will ever compliment your homework, but we've seen the doctors's faces, amazed at how you overcome adversities.

- We didn't have to dress you up for United Nations Day at school, but that day, you met more people from different cultures than we could ever imagine, right here at this hospital.

- I couldn't get you that enormous Mickey piñata I was planning on getting "when we got out," but we immensely value being together as a family and we celebrate what's really important: YOUR LIFE, without anything deflecting attention from it.

- In other ways, we received the greatest gift there is: LIFE in the form of white blood cells that people have donated nonstop.

- We can't go out or enjoy the outdoors, but we have a giant window in this room that lets us see how life goes on out there, and it encourages us to do our best and wait for the moment we can go back there.

- We can't have playdates, but you have so many friends praying that you can play with them soon.

- It doesn't matter if we're not attending weekly Mass for now. Here, we see God every day.

- We learned that winning and losing are not the same thing, and that we have to fight and work hard for the win, because that's what we want. In any other case I would've told you that it doesn't matter.

- We don't have to worry about you sleeping alone in your room.

- You're only two years old and you've already been in marathons, biked for miles, you've climbed mountains, you've been an Ironman, you have medals and you've even skydived. You did all that through all those people that do it in your name.

You are what every kid dreams to be: A REAL SUPERHERO.

I can't say this has been the BEST year like many parents say when their children celebrate a birthday, what I can say is that although it could have been the WORST year ever, it really wasn't, and I'm sure that the worst part is over.

I would be lying if I said that I wouldn't trade it for ANYTHING, but I can tell you that we've changed EVERYTHING to give you many more years.

We would be more comfortable at home, in our country... But I can't thank God enough for letting us have you here and now.

We've given up EVERYTHING so that we don't have to give YOU up.

I can't promise you that EVERYTHING will get BETTER, but I can assure you that we're doing our BEST to make it better.

I WISH that this coming year is a year of victory and complete health, I want to celebrate you every year of my life... I have faith, and I've never lost it, that a great year is ahead of us.

God is allowing us to start this year without complications, and boy, did we have some!

HAPPY FIRST TWO YEARS OF MANY MORE TO COME! I'm so proud of you, you've accomplished what many people can't do in a lifetime.

Thank you #LPAP for being my great little teacher at only two years old.

👍 689   💬 91   ➤

NEUROSURGERY

Good morning sunshine!

Since the news of the fungus disappearing, we haven't had any more good news. We are still in the battle. The doctors keep looking and finding.

The oncologist told us that one of the scans they did while trying to figure out what had happened with the fungal infection, showed a whirl of cancerous cells in your brain. You will have to have a surgery where they will put a valve inside your head to administer chemo directly into your brain. Because of your current condition, with a weakened immune system and low platelets, the ones in charge of healing wounds, this is a very serious surgery and it has to be done soon. Today, you had a platelets transfusion again since they don't want to take any chances. I feel anxious, but I have been quite calm, considering. We are in God's hands.

In other news, your catheter got infected, the one that is hooked to your heart, making all the medicines and chemo reach your bloodstream. They had to poke your arm several times to put a new one in, your veins are very damaged and there are not many to choose from. The VAT team had to come with this machine similar to an ultrasound to find your veins, and even with that they had a hard time finding one. Your arm was so damaged that they had to put a metal brace and strap it up, which makes it really uncomfortable when you are trying to sleep, but you don't complain, you make everything easier and I will be forever grateful for that.

Tomorrow morning you will have the surgery. I'll write you later.

 Nayeli Pereznegrón
November 10, 2014

Well, we have an update on the cancerous cells they found in Luis Pablo's head. It's a turmoil, and instead of decreasing, the doctors are seeing more. That's why they decided to resort to surgery.

In the following days, Luis Pablo will have **NEUROSURGERY** to have a small valve placed in his brain. This valve will be connected to a vein that feeds all the others, and will release chemotherapy in the area that concerns us. We all know any brain-related matter is very serious and the fact that Luis Pablo will be going in with a depleted immune system and very low platelets, even after the transfusion, only makes it even more complicated.

As soon as we know the date and time of the surgery we will let you know for you to join us in prayer.

Thank you for your prayers, please keep them coming!

👍 4205   💬 335   ↗

Nayeli Pereznegrón
November 6, 2014

My sister showed me some of the messages you leave here and I am deeply thankful. Again, my apologies because we can't answer them all.

Two messages drew my attention today: One, from a leukemia foundation that said they use this page to encourage other moms that are going through the same thing; and another one from a young lady, telling me she was doubting what her future was, but she decided to go to nursing school after she read about Luis Pablo.

I also got a beautiful letter from a future doctor, telling Luis Pablo he wants to become an oncologist after hearing his story. Another one from a seminarian telling Luis Pablo that every morning he offers his day for him. He tells him what he means to so many people and he talks beautifully about God.

Just today, the day I heard so many bad news, I'm also getting some good news, all of the above.

And not just that, doctors from LPAP's medical team, and doctors that are not on the team but that have seen Luis Pablo for some other reasons, came to show their support, as well as all the nurses. Even one of the infectious diseases doctors that only saw him when he had the fungus was here, she cried, hugged me and told me she would be praying for him. Everybody loves Luis Pablo.

These are all tiny little miracles among all this adversity and uncertainty... God keeps proving Himself.

I have no words to thank all your love and support!

I will try to go to sleep tonight with this image in my mind, very important for our family. I know many others have donated, and many more have given their time to find out if they're a match. I know many of you have spent many hours donating, and more than once, but these are the only pictures that we have.

Every night when Luis Pablo is praying he says: "Thank you for my angels on earth that are giving me life." LPAP has you in his blood - literally.

May God bless each and every one of those who have been with us one way or the other, during this extremely difficult stage of our lives.

👍 4356   💬 196   ➔ 67

Some of the many donors for Luis Pablo.

You had your surgery today. It took a while but everything is fine. Now you have this little ball coming out of your head, and that is where they will put the chemo. I don't even want to think how that will go.

You came out in good spirits, like usual. This time, when I noticed you were waking up, I stood very close to your face, you opened your eyes and I stuck my tongue out. You smiled and said "coquito" as you call your coconut water, my heart was torn in two, I tried to distract you and I started singing, but you were so weak and remained silent. I kept singing, then you looked at me and thanked me with those big bright eyes of yours, one of the most beautiful facial expressions you have, and you asked for your iPad. We watched Pocoyo until they took us back to your room. You were not in the mood for talking and I always try to give you space when you need it.

Back in the room, after you ate and you were in better spirits, I told you what had happened.

"Now you have a tablet on your head," I said. "Like those colorful ones we like to eat... Yummy!"

"Mmm... Yummy!" you replied.

"Yes, and it is magical! Sometimes they will put some medicine there and it will make it taste better. Do you remember when we talked about your food tasting like the magnets on the fridge? Well, we're trying to avoid that from happening."

Luis Pablo after his surgery.

104

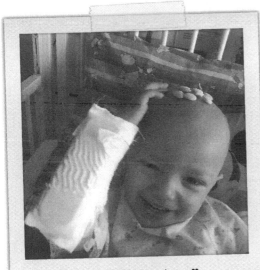

Luis Pablo showing off his colorful tablets for his chemotherapy.

"Lemon?" you asked. "Yes! Lemon, strawberry, and grape! Do you want to see it?" "Yes!"

"Okay, but first we are going to put more tablets there so that you can see."

I quickly filled the top of your head with some colorful candy that I had bought while you were in the OR. I showed you with the cellphone camera, and when you saw yourself, you started laughing so hard. I was able to take a picture right there! I was laughing out loud too.

Tomorrow morning they will give you the first chemo.

Like always, I surrender to God's arms and put you in his hands, asking Him to handle your pain and my heart's pain. By the way, how does my heart beat for you?

Here is the picture I took when you had the tablets on your head, and you can see the brace I was telling you about.

⎯⎯ᴠ♡₂ᴸ⎯⎯

This morning they gave you the first chemo in your head and it was traumatic for me to see it. It seems like it is not a procedure they do often. A group of doctors came in to observe.

Mateo has joined your medical staff, a doctor that is just beginning his medical journey. He has a big heart and a bright mind, he always smiles when he is with you. I can tell you hold a special place in his heart and it is hard for him to hide it. Imagine his affection for you that when he traveled to China, he brought you an amulet for health and good luck.

With the doctors surrounding your bed, they put some lidocaine on the tablet you have on your head. After 30 minutes, they inserted a needle there. I was lying next to you, holding you tight in my arms while dad held your legs so that you didn't move and to avoid an accident. We were surprised to see that when you felt the needle entering your head, you just closed your eyes tightly. They injected the chemotherapy, took the needle out, put a bandage, and only one tear rolled down your face. We're all amazed by you!

"All done, Luis Pablo," the doctor said with misty eyes, after witnessing your bravery.

"A la bio.. a la bao.." You asked for your chant, the one we always sing as a cheer after you do something we know is hard.

"Bravo, *Pavito*! You did great!" Your dad started.

"Ra, ra, raaa…" You finished.

I also sang the chant. I was smiling but my heart was broken into a million pieces. We are going to do this everyweek, I beg God to give us strength and I thank Him for the chance of being by your side. Tomorrow is your dad's birthday and I am waiting for you to go to sleep now so I that can decorate the room and have everything ready for tomorrow.

We celebrated dad's birthday today, that wonderful man thagave you life and for whom I thank God every day for having by my side. He is our cornerstone and strength in these moments. For his gift, we got him a sweater just like the one you were wearing today when you welcomed him singing Happy Birthday. I don't know

Luis Pablo and his dad, twinning.

which of you was more surprised when you found out you both had the same outfit. He is your hero and you were very happy to be dressed like him.

We had a special day filled with love in your little hospital room. Dad has to go back to work tomorrow, he has neglected everything because of us, but thank God we can have him next to us. While he is away, your auntie Ale will stay here. We have a good thing going, but still, it's not the same without your dad here. I try not to show my fears when he leaves to make the load easier on him.

Dad left already and something strange happened that night. We had the same bedtime routine as always: You made space for me in your crib and we said our prayers. After that, I started singing a lullaby that you always hum along until you fall asleep and you don't wake up until the next morning. But today, you woke up shortly after I sang the lullaby, and you were laughing. I didn't know what was happening and I didn't want you to see me, so I just took a peek trying to be as careful as possible. I saw you, you were sitting in your crib as if you were trying to catch butterflies, I think that is the best way to describe it. It was very strange because there was nothing there and it was three in the morning. You were just there, laughing trying to catch something. I thought you were sleepwalking, and I was able to come closer and record a video on my phone. I asked you what you were doing and you just kept laughing and smiling and making the same movement, after a while you laid down and fell sound asleep.

CHRISTMAS SEASON

We went over your vocabulary flashcards like we do every morning. I took a video of you so you can watch it some day and be amazed of yourself, like I am, for having such an impressive vocabulary at such a young age. I think spending all this time together has contributed to it, but sometimes I can't help but be amazed that all that chemo, the anesthesia and medicine they have put directly in your head haven't impacted your brainpower. It is a miracle.

After breakfast, they moved us to another room. We change rooms every two or three months. I hate to do this because I have to pack all of our stuff, but I know it is a good thing because we get a fully sterilized room.

Rooms are assigned randomly and we go to whichever room we get. They are almost all the same and I never complain. But there is one I really like because it's bigger. It is a corner room and it has an extra space that is amazing. The bonus space is designated for hospital storage, but it is almost always empty.

I will try to explain it better. On the outside you have two big purple doors that open to a space no larger than 9 ft., at least that is what dad says, because when he is bored, he just walks around measuring spaces with steps. On the left, there is a regular door that opens to a standard room that measures around 180 sq. ft.

Since we are not seeing any improvement, it is almost a given that we will spend Christmas here. That is why I thought about that room, because in case you are not feeling well on Christmas Eve, you can stay asleep and we can still spend time with whoever wants to join us, since there will be no restrictions for visitors that day. But still, we will be cautious and only invite our immediate family. I begged the nurses to get us that room, that is why this time it took them longer to move us, because they were waiting for our favorite room to free up. Once it became available, they happily let us know our room was ready. I love them!

After we settled in our new room, I asked your aunt Ale to watch you while I went out to buy some Christmas decorations. I have always loved the Christmas season. When your dad and I were newlyweds, we still needed a bunch of things for our house, but our Christmas decor was in full swing. This time, we will have less decorations but I still want to create a special atmosphere in your room.

We have been listening to Christmas music and you already learned Rudolph the Red Nosed Reindeer. There is a very cute video of you singing that song while you touch the scar on your head. I want to have everything ready before your auntie's birthday on December 3, tomorrow I will be in full on decorating mode. I bought a small Christmas tree and a nativity set, some ornaments, two nutcrackers, and a Mickey Mouse train set that I will put on the desk next to the window where the tree will be. I also got a lot of paper to decorate the doors, we have a lot of time to get crafty while we are here! I am so excited and can't wait to decorate your room, I want everything to look nice.

Christmas is almost here and I can't contain the joy I am feeling. I am so grateful that God has given us the chance of spending one more Christmas with you. The magic of the season is everywhere,

I have never felt it like this before. I believe it is all the angels on this floor that make it even more special, something hard to describe.

Dad arrived to spend his Christmas break with us, so you are in a great mood now. The effect he has on you is amazing. He renews your energy, and honestly, mine too. Ale is still here, and *Nana* and your grandparents got

Our Christmas room is ready.

here as soon as the break started. Grandma Malicha will join us too, she will spend Christmas with you in the hospital. Your uncles and aunts don't have their traveling visas ready yet, so we will miss them very much, especially your dad who was hoping to spend such a difficult and special Christmas with all our family. But I am sure next year you will be healthy and we will all be together watching you jump and run around.

I have something to tell you: You are kind of famous. Here at the hospital, in Houston, and in Mexico. At the beginning of November, we were contacted by a charitable foundation here in the United States to let us know they wanted to sponsor you. They have this program where families sign up and around Christmas time, they fulfill a wish list for kids and parents. I told them I appreciated the gesture, but since we really didn't need the help, they should pick another family. And that is the truth, we have the most important thing: YOU, and you have the most important thing: YOUR FAMILY.

I can't overstate how nice they were trying to convince me to let ourselves be pampered and telling me I shouldn't feel bad. I was a little embarrassed but I ended up accepting their offer. I kept thinking of things to write on the list and nothing came to mind, we knew they wouldn't get us everything on the list, only the things they could.

I asked you what you wanted for Christmas and (no wonder) you said a Mickey Mouse. You also asked for a glow in the dark race track, just like the one another boy in the hospital has. I wrote down that I wanted a very soft blanket for those cold nights at the hospital. I haven't had a chance to get one and I really need it. I also asked for some warm slippers and dad asked for a sweatshirt and some pajama pants

On the delivery day, three men and a woman knocked on

Luis Pablo's family getting presents of love and kindness.

112

our door with their hands filled with wrapped presents. The biggest one said BELIEVE, that word that means so much to us. You can imagine our surprise when we found out that besides getting us every thing on our list, they also got us an air purifier and a $500 gift card! Their generosity was unbelievable! Dad's eyes filled with tears.

"Thank you so much! We didn't want you to get us anything because we thought we didn't need it, but today I learned a great lesson, that we all need to accept some love once in a while, and that's what I feel today, love and kindness. Knowingthat someone was thinking of us and took the time to carefully pick each item, and giving us much more than what we asked for," your dad told them.

I have always been surrounded by love, but today, I felt special. They made me feel good and happy, I am very grateful. We all need to feel loved, I know material things are not important, but it is one way to make someone feel special.

 Nayeli Pereznegrón
November 12, 2014

Today has been an extremely tiring day. LPAP fasted the whole day, then we went to the OR but he was sent back. He had three platelets transfusions and still he couldn't meet the levels needed to go to surgery. Tomorrow at 7:30 a.m. he will have his surgery, it looks like his blood and platelets levels are now ready.

One of the doctors that we love and respect came to let us know that cancerous cells are still showing in Luis Pablo's body. He doesn't think chemo is working or that it ever will. When we asked him if he thought we would make it to transplant, he said NO. When we asked him if he had ever seen a child like Luis Pablo suddenly get better he also said NO. He told us we could decide not to have the surgery, since he doesn't think the chemo he's having through the valve is doing any improvements.

His words reminded me of the explanation we got when Luis Pablo had the fungal infection. It was a painful day, but we thank God because He is always present. All of a sudden we got a call from our main oncologist (who's out of town) and when we told her what they've told us, she explained:

"Luis Pablo is considered a high risk case. The possibilities of him not making it to transplant are higher. With Luis Pablo there is no plan A, B, or C, there is no protocol, his cancer is stronger than we can imagine, but if I thought we've run out of options, I would let you know. When talking about Luis Pablo we have to consider his entire history, he's a strong kid, and he's clinically stable to keep fighting."

I was very surprised by her following words: "When the fungus appeared, NONE of us thought he would make it, we thought it was over, and suddenly he bounced back. I think he deserves a chance. I've had worse cases where they miraculously recover."

If we want to talk numbers, we have a less than 20% chance of surviving this, or so we've been told. But for us, that 20% represents hope, and we can't give up after fighting for so long. Like we told the doctor that didn't give us any hopes, when he asked if we would consent to tomorrow's surgery or if we wanted to stop:

Our mission as parents is to make our children happy. Stopping would mean to go back home with a sick Luis Pablo, without medicine that would make him feel better, and even worse, with a family in despair. Would all that really help to make him happy? Luis Pablo is happy when his parents are by his side, when we love him and when we sing, that's the only thing he cares about. That love will continue to fight right beside him because it would have decided to stop when they thought everything was lost due to a fungus, we wouldn't be here today hearing these words, we would've never seen him get better, we wouldn't appreciate more than ever that we can watch him laugh, sing, and play. We would've taken a beaten Luis Pablo, and now we have the happy Luis Pablo back.

We're still leaving everything in God's hands and we will keep on fighting for as long as Luis Pablo is fighting, and believe me, it's amazing how this superhero won't give up and how he finds the strength to stay strong even after the prognosis he's facing.

WE ASK YOU TO PRAY NOW MORE THAN EVER! WE'LL GO FROM ONE SMALL MIRACLE TO THE NEXT UNTIL WE REACH THE GREAT MIRACLE!

Every house needs pebbles to be finished!

386   37   4

The amount of messages with prayers and good vibes we got after I posted that is impressive. You know what? I don't feel so alone like I used to when I first started this diary. First of all because I have God, you, and all our family, but also because I feel all these people walking beside us. It is hard to explain, they really make it seem like they are worried about a member of their own family. My mind still can't process all this love, I am so moved by it.

**Love and support for Luis Pablo
and his parents.**

Nayeli Pereznegrón
December 1, 2014

I couldn't sleep yesterday, I was feeling anxious and uneasy. So many thoughts were going through my head, my heart and my mind are not in the same channel.

My heart thinks that everything will be alright, but then my head tells me "don't get your hopes up" and the doctors' words only make it worse: "It's very complicated, our chances are very low."

While I was tossing and turning, from the core of my being I asked God to show Himself to me, that I needed Him more than ever, that my sorrow was strong and I wasn't sure if we were making the right choices about Luis Pablo's treatment. I wasn't sure if putting Luis Pablo through this was worth it, I don't know what's the best thing for him, what he would want us to do.

Well, today after weeks of laying on his bed all the time, without wanting to do anything, he woke up and welcomed me with the biggest smile, asking me to sing for him. Shortly after, a person from a charitable foundation that goes around with a cart delivering gifts for the children, handed me an angel and said: "I think this belongs to you, it would look really nice in this room."

I don't believe in coincidences but I do believe in Godincidences.

I'm amazed how He always shows himself to us.

CHRISTMAS IS HERE! Our gift to you was a full size Pocoyo costume, and boy did you like it! Your excitement is so pure and real! You are so happy because now Mickey and Pocoyo can come and visit you whenever you want, this has lifted your spirits. It is such a joy to watch you hug him! You were so thrilled that you fell asleep. Lately, you get tired more easily.

This afternoon, we heard some horrible news. A doctor that is not on your team but that was on-call, came to examine you and he asked your dad and me to step out of the room to talk. We went to the small room where they always give us the worst news. The moment we started heading there, I knew something bad was coming.

"This chemo round is over and Luis Pablo's cancer persists," he said.

"Okay, what's next?" Your dad asked.

"I'm going to be very honest here, we can continue chemotherapy, those never end, but the one who's going to be done is your son. If I were you, I would take him home to try to enjoy whatever life he has left."

I could feel my blood rushing and I started crying.

Luis Pablo and
his best Christmas present ever.

"That's not going to happen," your dad told him. "We will keep on fighting for as long as he keeps on fighting. Plus, if we decided to do that, how long do you think he has left?"

"You see, it's hard to know, but since his cancer is progressing so fast, I would say two or three weeks, a month at the most."

"Well, you'd better start looking at more options because we're not giving up. Thank you doctor, Merry Christmas," your dad said upset and headed towards the door.

I ran to him, grabbed his hand and hugged him while I cried.

"Don't worry, *chaparrita*, God will grant us this miracle, don't lose faith. I'm going to make some calls and I'll meet you in the room later."

I knew he was not going to call anybody, he just needed some space to let it all out without me watching.

Before entering your room, I took a deep breath, wiped away my tears and built up some courage. Your grandma and aunt were listening and singing along to the song "*Mi cachito.*" The moment you saw me, you got all excited and asked me to carry you. Something just didn't make sense when I saw those eyes full of life, so cheerful, so expressive. I couldn't believe what I had just heard. But I knew I could lose you soon, and that feeling I couldn't control. I felt it deep in my heart and the most unbearable sorrow took over me as I was holding you, with your bald little head on my cheek.

"What happened, Naye? What did they tell you?" My mom asked.

I couldn't answer. My eyes filled with tears and I just kept singing the song that was playing on the back, feeling the deepest pain in my soul. With tears in my eyes and my voice cracking, I sang:

"Mi cachito, mi pedazo de angelito, mi cachito mi pedazo de huracán…"

("My tiny chunk of angel, my tiny chunk of a hurricane.")

You pouted and your eyes started to get teary, too. The moment I sang the verse "whenever you want me to, I will always hug you…" you said "NOW."

I held you against my chest and you started bawling, they were tears of sorrow connected to mine.

We were together in a way that has no explanation, feeling the same pain, the desperation, fear, and uncertainty. I didn't have to say anything, we have such a strong connection that you felt it. My mom and sister were crying too, watching in awe and impressed at our strong connection. Without asking anything they understood what was going on just by watching us. Your aunt caught this moment on video, someday I will show it to you. Seeing it today hurts.

I am moved and impressed to see how you understand everything, you know more than me.

Your wisdom amazes me, scares me, and makes me tremble. It seems like it is a wisdom from someone who doesn't belong to this world. It pains me to write this, but that is what it feels like, especially today.

I don't want to write anything else, I just want to tell you that I will fight with you for as long as God will let us, and I will continue to live happily every day by your side. I will never give up, of that you can be sure.

And, how does my heart beat for you?

Nayeli Pereznegrón
December 25, 2015

On Christmas morning we got the biopsy results and it was not what we were hoping for. The percentage of leukemia is higher, which means neither the chemo nor the alternative treatment we've been using have worked or seem to be working against such an aggressive cancer. When the cancer came back, the levels were at 3%, after treatment, it has increased to over 70%. These are significant, serious, and important figures.

Luis Pablo was diagnosed with ACUTE MYELOID LEUKEMIA M7. The word leukemia by itself is already terrifying to anyone, but there are two types of leukemia: lymphoblastic and myeloid. Myeloid Leukemia is much more aggressive, it is less common in kids and there is not much research on this since the majority of its cases are on patients over 60 years old. Myeloid Leukemia is then divided in CHRONIC AND ACUTE. Chronic leukemia progresses more slowly, while an acute one progresses incredibly fast.

Then we have the subtypes, that go from M0 to M7. M7 is the worst of them all since it develops much more fibrosis than the others, making it extremely difficult to attack the cancer.

As you can see, since the beginning Luis Pablo was diagnosed with leukemia, the worst of its kind, the worst subtype, and the worst number. This diagnosis represents only 1% of ALL pediatric cancers in the world according to the American Society of Pediatric Cancer.

• • •

This is why I argue that statistics, percentages and numbers mean nothing when it comes to your child. Knowing all of this and after a relapse, why would we think it would be easy to beat it?

Of course we know we're facing something extremely difficult, impossible to some, but why would we settle with being only the 1% of such a horrendous diagnosis and not take the chance for a teeny-tiny possibility to turn it?

We were already given the bad, does that mean we don't get the good part?

For us, it's ALL OR NOTHING... If there is hope, no matter how small and as long as Luis Pablo is fit to do it, we will stay in this battle.

I'm always bringing up the time he was in the ICU with that fungal infection, because right there they were giving us almost no chance of making it according to the percentages, and miraculously, the fungus was gone in two weeks after we were told it would take over six months to get rid of it because his immune system was depleted.

Now we know why we never got a diagnosis during those three weeks we were in the hospital in Monterrey... Because it is so hard to figure out! We thank God for our pediatrician in Saltillo who acted fast, and for our oncologist and her team, the hospital, and nurses. It's because of them that we can keep on fighting.

The good news is that his organs are working perfectly besides all the poison. He plays, walks, laughs, sings and dances constantly! He continues to give us the strength to keep going.

He hasn't had any complications which continues to impress everybody. These are the little miracles God is doing for us, little by little. His brain is still under control, the chromosome mutation remains low. He is unbelievably strong, every child fighting this battle is, but LPAP leaves me speechless... You would never guess his diagnosis by looking at him.

We had a wonderful Christmas. We started early, at around 6 p.m., because we knew he wouldn't stay up for too long. I changed him into his outfit that we carefully picked for him knowing he would only wear it once, but it didn't matter, we wanted him to look handsome and elegant. We went for a walk around the hallway, I was taken by surprise because he got really tired, he didn't want to open any gifts and just wanted to go to sleep. He didn't eat his dinner, I went to tuck him in while the rest of the family stayed in the small area that we decorated beautifully, the area was cozy and music was playing at a low volume to respect our neighbors. After he fell asleep I went to the other room to have dinner, I was sad because I'd planned everything for him to enjoy and my soul wished that he could spend at least a few minutes with us.

When we finished our dinner, we opened our gifts and Luis Pablo suddenly woke up. I went to pick him up and he asked me to bring him with the others, his mood had changed! He was a totally different kid! He sat on my lap, opened his gifts, he danced, sang, laughed, and played with us. It was just one hour that made our whole Christmas worth it. We are extremely grateful for having this Christmas. We spent the night with him and in the morning he asked to sit on the sofa with us, we cuddled there for a while. For sure one meaningful and special Christmas, that's what we'll keep our focus on, THE GOOD AND THE POSITIVE, because just as there's a lot of bad, there's also a lot of good. We don't feel defeated with this news, we're still standing with hope and faith, taking in every moment with our child and accepting God's will, but begging from the bottom of our hearts that his will is to leave him here with us. We are so thankful for the family that joined us on this very special Christmas, and missing those that are far away, you're always in our prayers.

MERRY CHRISTMAS FROM OUR LITTLE FAMILY!

THANK YOU TO HIS CLASSMATES FOR KEEPING HIM IN YOUR THOUGHTS. I KNOW HE WILL BE THERE WITH YOU SOON!

👍 13 mil   💬 1.8 mil   ➤ 511

Luis Pablo and his family
enjoying Christmas together.

NEW YEAR, NEW HOPE

Pavito, we are here together celebrating the arrival of a new year. My parents and sister are about to leave. You are going to miss Nana so much, you two play and argue like siblings. Being with her and your grandparents is so good for you.

Your grandma Abu left a few days ago. You gave her so much love. I'm proud and impressed that even though you don't see her that often, you know her well and love her so much.

Since we learned on Christmas day that besides the chemo and other treatments, your cancer continues to grow. I have been studying day and night, and with the help of Dr. Mateo, I made a map of every chemo block you've had since you started treatment.

We divided everything by blocks and I wrote down the name of the substance each chemo had, as well as your blood count and lab results you had after each of them to determine which ones had the most effect on you and which ones didn't work. I found out you have had over 250 chemotherapies. What you have endured is really impressive.

The map is hanging from the room's windows. Every day I am crossing out and adding more information. When nurses and staff notice it, they ask what it is. I just tell them it is all the chemo you've had.

The desk used to be covered with toys, but now there is a bunch of papers of the medical history and treatments they have used in other kids with your same type of leukemia. I have analyzed every combination and compared it with what they have used in you. Everything has notes on red ink and highlighter. I have turned to some doctors for help when there is something I don't understand or that Google can't explain. I have printed medical trials from hospitals in Philadelphia, Memphis, and Boston. I know there is talk in the hospital about what I am doing. They probably think I am crazy. I don't judge them because I sometimes think that too, but I can't take NO for an answer. The doctors are way too busy and see so many patients that they don't have the time to make a thorough investigation like what I am doing.

At this point in the battle, no other hospital would take you in, that is why I am trying to find something positive in my research. I am reading when I wake up and I am reading when I go to bed, I am doing everything I can. I will always do everything in my power to keep you here, to hug you and tuck you in every night.

Happy New Year! You can probably tell what is the thing I wish with all my heart.

And, how does my heart beat for you?

ETOPOSIDE! That word came to my mind when I woke up. The night before, I fell asleep studying trials and chemo routes. It is January 5 and the doctors are already back from their break, so the answer was right on time. Dr. Mateo and I went through all the maps I made. We discussed it and decided Etoposide could be a good options to get you to remission.

I desperately asked to speak with Dr. Dreyer who called as soon as she could. I told her about my research and my discoveries. Turns out she was not giving up either and was already considering other chemo routes. When she came in the room she was amazed by the length and accuracy of my investigation. There, I showed her every route we have used, every lab result that was promising, all the trials that had worked in kids like you. All in all to explain why I thought Etoposide could be a good option.

"Using a previously used chemo is not good because cancer usually recognizes it," she said.

"I know, but we've tried everything and it seems like nothing is working. Luis Pablo has had great results when he's had it and one of the papers that I read showed a trial in Boston where a child got into remission even after retaking the drug."

You could see the doubt in her face, but she knew there were not a lot of options left.

"Let's try it," she said, trying not to dismiss my effort. "I will look for a route that could work using Etoposide."

I hugged her with a big smile on my face and told her: "I am not a doctor and I don't pretend to be one, but when I learned everything was lost I couldn't accept that and I decided to do something else. If this doesn't work, at least I will know that I did everything I could to try to find something and that I didn't just stand there. Again, we have nothing to lose."

Celia and her son, Juanito, have become my family in this hospital. She has been fighting her son's leukemia for a long time and her faith in God is impressive. Talking to her has a positive impact on me. She is the one who told me about the healing prayer we always say at night: "Jesus have mercy on him, Jesus heal him, Jesus free him." She has no idea, but every time we say that prayer, it brings us peace.

One day, she told me about a man with a special spiritual gift that had once visited her child, and that while he was praying, some incredible things had happened. She told me we should have him visit you. I don't usually like people giving me suggestions, but she is different, so I listened to her.

The man was here today. He is a Hispanic man that struggled to read, but his presence brought to our room something I can't explain. When he got here, he talked to you, hugged you, touched your forehead, and started praying. I closed my eyes as I felt so much love in the air. I was really focused on my prayer when suddenly a strong smell of roses took over the room. I didn't know where it was coming from, I opened my eyes and everybody else was still praying.

"Am I going crazy, here?" I started questioning myself. "Why am I smelling this? Am I the only one?".

Your dad had left the room, and when he came back and opened the door he said:

"What's with the flower smell? What kind of perfume did you spray?"

"You notice the smell of roses, too?" my sister asked.

"Yes," I replied.

The man then said: "Virgin Mary is holding him, you have nothing to worry about."

When he left, Luis walked him out the door to say goodbye. I stayed with Celia in the room.

"I told you friend, he's special," she said. "I experienced that same smell of roses in my son's room, I was surprised to hear you talk about that."

We didn't talk much about it, but we were very impressed. It was a magical and indescribable moment, but once the excitement was gone, I started reasoning, I couldn't sleep that night thinking about an explanation for that smell. My dad taught me to always find a reason for things, that nothing happens magically. I thought he might had a perfume that he sprayed when we all closed our eyes, or maybe he uses some sort of oil on his hands. I feel bad for thinking that he could be playing a trick on us, but there must be something to justify that smell. Maybe I will figure it out on his next visit.

The man with the spiritual gift came to visit again today. I promised myself I wouldn't close my eyes, not even for a second. I had to see everything.

He started praying and quickly after, the smell of roses was there. I observed everything around me. Luis and my sister were praying, you were smiling looking at the ceiling, the man kept praying. I stood next to him and grabbed his hands. Dismissing my embarrassment, I smelled them. I couldn't help it, I thought he had used something with that fragrance, but to my surprise, his hands smelled like nothing and my nose could definitely notice the scent. I gave up right there and I admitted that I didn't need an explanation, what I was experiencing was very simple and I was trying to make it complicated. God and the Virgin Mary were present there, I cried and asked forgiveness for not believing like I said I would.

Right before going to bed, your dad told me that night:

"I wish you could put into words what we experienced today, it was a ver special moment and you have a gift for that."

"I wish I could," I answered, making him think that I wouldn't do it. I feel bad for not trying, but it is something so personal and hard to describe.

Also, every time I heard about things like that, something inside me wonders if it is really true. I know I am being silly because God gave me a great gift when He let me experience that, but talking about this is complicated. That is why I am only writing this for you.

I don't want to forget this, and I hope I am able to describe it to you someday when you can understand the miracle we had through you. And the feeling of peace that I can't explain. The two times he was here, I felt as if I was sedated. I felt so airy, so comfortable, so happy, so relaxed.

We started another round of chemo with Etoposide and a whole army of prayers on social media. People are aware that this is probably our last chance of getting a transplant, your last and only chance to beat cancer.

It will be four days of intense chemo. We are hoping your count will go up without the cancer increasing so that we can take the next step. Here we go again! With faith and hope that everything will be okay! Auntie Tati came to help us and she has been alternating with Ale to stay with you some nights. It definitely helps you to have new faces around here, it boosts you up.

Nayeli Pereznegrón
January 27, 2015

Today marks a year since we started this battle. Five months since Luis Pablo was admitted after his relapse. Today, a whole year later, they told us Luis Pablo didn't make it to remission, the cancer recognized the drug. He is still happy, smiling and joyful as always. His organs are perfectly fine.

A week ago I told you about how happy I was because Juanito was finally going to get his transplant, I've asked a lot of prayers for him. Him and Luis Pablo started this journey together, Celia and I have become really close during this relapse, last week we prayed together and we experienced things like we've never had before. We felt lucky to be feeling God's presence so close to us. Celia has given me my faith back every time I need it. And just today, they told them the cancer is back too, different doctors were giving us the same news at the same time. Funny thing is that they suggested the same treatment, for the first time in their battles, they will have the same chemo. The risks are high, we will be together against the same enemy and using the same weapons, and most importantly having faith that they both will get through this. I believe God is working and guiding two different doctors who are using the same medicines for two diagnosis that are similar but at the same time, very different. The strength comes in numbers, and together with your prayers and good vibes we will soon have a miracle done in our children. Juanito and Luis Pablo are definitely quite the case in this hospital, their outlooks are the same. We are two families that are together in this.

With tears in our eyes we hugged each other today, we couldn't believe we were getting the same news after having such strong experiences in our faiths, but we agree that God has a perfect plan and that because of Him we can go on and that our children are still standing.

Our doctor, who is a very smart and renowned person, as well a huge blessing for us, told me today: "Many could think we are crazy for opting to continue treatment, but they haven't met Luis Pablo." He continues to amaze us... and there's nothing more. He keeps on fighting, keeps playing, and keeps asking us to take him to Mickey Mouse's house when he's out of here.

If he still believes he can, who are we to tell him he can't?

We are asking for all the prayers for Juanito and Luis Pablo, as well as for us, their families, we've been in this hospital for too long, with a roller-coaster of emotions, a continuous fight, it is impossible not to be tired. I am always asking for prayers for Luis Pablo and Juanito, but this time, please include their families: their grandparents, aunts, uncles, and those who have been impacted by this diagnosis. Also, pray for those who have hurt us with negative messages, and from the bottom of our hearts, thank you to those who keep supporting us with prayers, donations, time, and well-wishes. All of you who have not given up hoping for a miracle.

Like I always say, with our feet on the ground, but with our eyes on the sky.

Here we go again! As many times as we need because God already gave us a miracle: our children!!!

👍 5.1 mil   💬 730   ➤ 160

Nayeli Pereznegrón
January 6, 2015

Hello! The first white blood cell donor (my husband) is scheduled for tomorrow. That means today they will call everybody on the list to schedule their appointment, since we need many donors. There are no words to thank you for your support and generosity, like they say: Nobody fights alone.

One of the donors who donated twice last time was telling me about the process. I got chills when I heard: "When I was donating the blood cells I was thinking: Please God, make these cells go to the right place and let them fight the fungus, let these cells give Luis Pablo all the energy he needs to continue fighting."

I think all those good vibes worked. I'm sure everybody who donated was thinking of Luis Pablo, as well as all of us that are not able to donate but are in constant prayer. You must know that the white blood cells are sometimes rejected, in fact, they're rejected most of the time, but thank God that never happens with Luis Pablo.

As I've said before, my boy carries inside of him a small piece of all his donors, thanks to them, and the prayers and good vibes he keeps smiling and fighting. He won't let you down!

Yesterday they had to remove his central line (the catheter inserted by surgery) because they found a bacteria, so they had to prick him twice to put two temporary lines for the antibiotics. They did this while I was not there, I've been away for two days. I haven't been feeling well and my throat hurts, and as you know, even the smallest virus could be FATAL for a child with a depleted immune system. This is the first time I have to stay here resting. Thank goodness my husband and sister are still here and are taking good care of Luis Pablo, I know he's in great hands.

After 16 days together, my parents and my other sister left. For 16 days they did everything and I was able to rest. I think this is why I got sick, haha, I'm not used to being this relaxed.

Now that I'm away from LPAP and without any distractions, I'm realizing how much emotionally dependent I am. For a year I've been entirely devoted to him. He's my son, my job, my companion, my friend, my distraction, my weekend plans, my gym, my coffee outing, my going to the movies. Everything I used to do without him, now I do with him only, and when someone invites me to "get my mind off things" it's no longer than two hours before I start to get impatient wanting to go back to the hospital or checking in with whoever is watching him.

If I go somewhere, I'm thinking about him all the time, he's my only vice.

We've been living together inside these four walls, where we've experienced joys, sorrows, fantasies, and confinement. And where we've learned a lot and created such a special connection, so special that when I'm singing a song that hits me hard, even though he's two years old and doesn't understand the words, he hugs me and starts crying with me. That's why even if he's terrified of going in the "time machine" to get some x-rays, he does it because he knows I will be right next to him.

I can tell when he's going to have a fever two hours before the nurses confirm it, I know when he's going to feel nauseous, by looking at him when he wakes up I can tell if he's going to have a good or a bad day. We've spent so much time together that I feel we're ONE. I miss him so much, but I'm taking my antibiotic and doing all the home remedies I know, because I want to go back, back to that world that we will soon leave and we will never miss. but a world that we've made ours so that LP can be as happy as it gets.

As always, please keep praying for him. Thank you for your support, donations, prayers, and words of encouragement! It helps us so much!

👍 4.3 mil   💬 380   ➦ 86

Hello *Pavo*, we have been apart and I miss you badly, but you don't miss me as much. You are so happy to spend time with other people. I am using these days to catch up on some personal and business issues. I am also going to get a hair cut, I can't remember the last time I had one, but I do remember the time a lady with really short hair was telling me in the playroom that she had shaved her head when her daughter with cancer had to do it, that is how she convinced her to do it, by "playing" they were getting a hair cut.

"How many warriors I've found on this floor!" I thought then.

I also thought it was a good thing you didn't pay attention to your hair because I wouldn't want to cut off my hair. I have always had long hair and I love it, but the other day I saw a post about a foundation that made wigs for girls out of donated hair. I couldn't resist, so I did it! I donated my hair! Here is my picture.

I shared this on a post on your Facebook group and I was amazed to see many positive feedback and the impact it had in so many people's hearts. Over 30 people cut their hair to donate it too, and they sent pictures. Some of them took it to a friend's beauty salon, and some of them sent their hair directly to me.

Nayeli Pereznegrón
January 20, 2015

I have to stop saying yes when I hear "It's to help children with cancer" but I feel I'm doing the right thing and it makes me happy, it's one of the few things you can do when it comes to cancer.

If you know me, you know how important my hair is for me. I take really good care of it (although lately I've been losing a lot of it) and it has been a big part of my personality, but I donated it today.

I'm glad I took such good care of it so that someone special can use it. I made the donation in Luis Pablo's name #lpap:

My mom would want to do way more for kids like you and me. This hair has been taken care of really well, never dyed, and treated with a lot of love because it is her favorite thing about her.

Because of girls like you, she learned that true beauty is not in the hair, and she would love it if somebody could donate to her some of the beauty, commitment, persistence, strength, and ability to fight that you have. It is an honor to give you a smile. With love, # LPAP.

What we can do to help is nothing compared to what these kids teach us.

#cancersucks #leukemiasucks #superheroes

👍 1.7 mil   💬 118   ➔ 33

134

You are in remission, Luis Pablo! It is amazing and I can't contain my joy! I am so grateful to God, the doctors, and all the people that prayed for you. After many many tests, we are moving floors today! We are going to the transplant floor, with filtered air, many restrictions, no visitors or volunteers, isolation, filters, double doors, sanitization and deep cleaning. And we are so happy to be headed over there! I never thought I would feel this excited about going to the transplant unit.

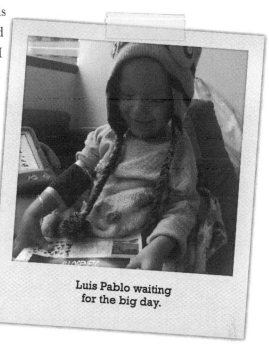

Luis Pablo waiting for the big day.

The medical team found an umbilical cord in Spain that is a 9 out of 10 match. The paperwork is done and it will get here on Wednesday. Once it gets here, we will begin preparations for your transplant. This is wonderful! I can't wait for a year to go by and meet the family that gave my son his life back. You will still need granulocytes, so I will have to post to social media hoping that a lot of people will donate since it is a critical requirement that you get daily white blood cell transfusions until the big day.

Nayeli Pereznegrón
March, 2, 2015

Hello. It's been a long and complicated weekend. Too many shots, I've never seen so many needles and injections, they kept looking and finding new things. We know we have a small window to go to transplant, that's why we worry when something comes up. The moment he got the white blood cells from the first donor, everything started to get better.

THANK YOU SO MUCH to all of you who have donated or are scheduled to do so. We have very bad reception in this room, but my sister showed me some of your messages and they brought tears to my eyes. On the donors' list I saw names of friends that have donated, two, three or more times, parents of other kids with cancer that met Luis Pablo, people that have been wanting to donate since we first asked back in August, people that got scared of the process but are willing to try again because they want to help, moms that look for specific time slots because they have to find a babysitter for their children, young people that stopped by before going to school or after leaving the office, even some that had to arrange transportation or don't speak the language figured out a way to do it. I could go on and on about so many beautiful messages. We really have no words to thank all of you, mainly our Hispanic community in Houston, your solidarity and unity have taught us a great beautiful lesson. I'm SO PROUD to be part of this community. THANK YOU FOR GIVING US SO MUCH! Luis Pablo is a very lucky kid.

THERE ARE SO MANY GOOD-HEARTED PEOPLE! If we saw more of the good stuff on the news, we would remember this more often. TOMORROW WE OFFICIALLY BEGIN THE TRANSPLANT TREATMENT. The bacteria finally eased up, although it doesn't mean it's gone completely, but we're getting ahead of this. Tomorrow they will do another central line on him to avoid so many injections. The countdown will go from 10 to 0. Day ZERO is TRANSPLANT DAY.

During those 10 days, they'll finish killing his marrow in order to transplant the new one. THESE WILL BE SOME CRITICAL HOURS, we ask you to join us in prayer.

Tomorrow we start a long journey, it's going to be a rollercoaster ride. As they say: Here comes the good stuff, hang on tight! And yes, we're hanging tight from God's hand who never lets us go.

WE WILL STILL NEED YOUR DONATIONS, before, during, and after transplant.

• • •

Please, if anybody wants to donate send a messagethat says POSSIBLE DONOR, please add your phone number and email. We will explain the process and if you agree, we will schedule a date.

You will be donating WHITE BLOOD CELLS, the ones that help our bodies fight viruses, infections, bacterias. LPAP needs a lot of them because he's going into battle without any of his own, and with a bacteria that has been defeated but not fully extinguished. There's also the possibility that his body is hosting a fungus, some virus, or leukemia, we don't really know because there is no time to do a biopsy. Plus, 10 antibiotics and some body organs protected by God that are in pristine condition even after 200 chemo sessions and more medicine that I can name. He's the "miracle boy" as the hospital staff calls him sometimes.

TOMORROW WE BEGIN A GREAT BATTLE, we're in God's hands and have the continuous support of our families, and two big armies of people praying and blood donors that fight every battle next to Luis Pablo, every day until his new bone marrow has recovered.

Plus we have on our side a new and amazing medical team, it was such a blessing meeting our new transplant doctor, a woman of God that speaks Spanish, we feel at peace and it is very clear God is acting through her.

INFINITE THANKS FOR SO MANY THINGS AND SO MUCH LOVE FOR LUIS PABLO!

THANK YOU FOR SO MANY SACRIFICES, SO MANY PRAYERS, AND ALL YOUR LOVE.

On Sunday we went to Mass here in Houston, where we don't know anyone, but one little girl walked over to us and said: "We're praying for Luis Pablo!" My heart shrunk, we have no idea of all the people that are asking for the same miracle as us. THANK YOU FROM THE BOTTOM OF OUR HEARTS.

👍 5.5 mil 💬 545 ➤ 236

Nayeli Pereznegrón
February 18, 2015

22 hours of fasting because they can't do this as an outpatient procedure like other children, he must go to the OR because he's had so many biopsies and one time he bled a lot, but anyway, finally in! Please keep the prayers and good vibes coming. Results won't be in until Friday. In God's name.

BONE MARROW TRANSPLANT

Welcome March!

Seven months after Luis Pablo's relapse and him being in the hospital the entire time, we finally made it to transplant. Thank God!

After we learned the process and care that a bone marrow transplant requires, your father and I agreed that I would go to Saltillo for a three-day break. He will stay with you, along with Ale and my mom. I am not comfortable leaving, but I need to recharge my energy for what's coming next, I know it won't be easy.

"If all of this has been difficult, you have no idea what a transplant means," a nurse told us.

To better deal with the intense days we will be facing, I will go to the ranch with your grandfather and I will try to unplug mentally and gather some strength because honestly, I am drained.

Once they explained all the risks you could face during and after the transplant, hospital administration made us sign a ton of papers, I just read them quickly, but I noticed it mentioned a great majority of bone marrow recipients become sterile. I have to confess it broke my heart, but there is nothing more important than your life, plus, miracles do happen! Technology advances at a crazy pace, and I have always thought adoption is a beautiful thing. Funny thing, your dad thought the exact same thing.

"Look, when everything goes back to normal we can start looking into adoption so that *Pavito* grows with that example and he can witness that not all children share their parents genetics but they become a family in ways that God has planned," I told him.

"Yes, you are completely right," he answered.

I don't want to get ahead of myself, but it makes me hopeful to think we could do it, time will tell, but once again, here you are, inspiring us.

 Nayeli Pereznegrón
February 26, 2015

Important!! Please share!! Houston peeps!! Granulocytes donation is vital for Luis Pablo. We're having a hard time and this is our ticket to transplant and to a lesser painful recovery. We need donors for an entire month! We need so many donors, they even let me donate too, finally!

If you're interested in helping, please know it is a three-day process and the hospital can work around your schedule.

Day 1. Appointment to donate platelets (around an hour and a half.)

Day 2. If you're compatible, the hospital will call to let you know you have to go back to the hospital to pick up a medicine you must inject yourself.

Day 3. White blood cell donations. The process takes about two hours.

In order to donate you must be in good health, not currently taking antibiotics or aspirins, not have had hepatitis, aids, or any other serious disease.

We have a long list that hasn't been of much help because when we call the possible donors to explain the process, a lot of them do not accept or they can't. We have to start a new list.

We are asking ALL of you willing to donate, whether you've written before or not, to send a message with the words POSSIBLE DONOR, please include your name and phone number to have the coordinator contact you and schedule your appointment.

I know we're asking you to do a lot for someone you may not know, but to fight this disease we need the support of a lot of people. What we wouldn't do to be able to do it all by ourselves, but since the beginning this has been a great team effort, including this beloved Facebook community. My sister is helping me with the new list. We're already in the transplant floor and reception is bad here.

May God bless you all for always helping us! You have no idea what every single cell you've donated means to us and to Luis Pablo. He made it here thanks to you and so many people. We will never be able to pay you back.

Don't forget to ask for your t-shit at the end. We encourage you to send your picture, we will save it for the superhero so that he never forgets and he can thank the support of so many people.

#localhero #save3lifes #giveblood #tacklecancer

👍 3.4 mil   💬 517   ➜ 2.8 mil

141

We started your pre-transplant chemo treatments eight days ago, that means we are in day -8. I haven't had much time to write and WiFi reception is very bad on this floor, so I haven't been able to talk to the people that are donating blood for you every day. Yes, Luis Pablo, people are still doing that for you, it is amazing, a true miracle. You know there are people out there giving you "soldiers" packed in plastic bags, which they give to you and the robot so that you can keep fighting.

Every time they are hanging a new bag you start growling like a lion and say "they're leaving" to the bad soldiers.

You will have your transplant on Friday 13, and from then we will count up, in positive numbers, and I am sure everything else will be positive too.

When I was talking about how thankful I am to the people that follow your page and how I try to keep them updated on your condition in return for their generosity, a mom from the hospital asked me: Up to which point?

And I wonder, up to which point can you thank somebody that prays every night for your child? Up to which point can you be grateful to the people that are donating life to him and that have to inject themselves some medication to donate white blood cells? Most of them we don't even know! Up to which point can you say thank you for offering 15 Masses for your son in 12 different cities? Up to which point can you be thankful to the people that took the time to write a letter and send a gift? Up to which point can you appreciate all the rosaries, sacrifices, and selfless acts they have done for him? Up to which point can I thank all the people that brings us food?

There is simply no point. There is no limit to be thankful! Sometimes I feel like I am not being grateful enough, but I know that some day you and I will be helping other kids with cancer, and that will be the best way to give back so much love and kindness.

You have been very quiet lately, you barely speak. This time you are getting a very strong chemo and you would rather be sleeping. When you wake up and you're happy, I play with you, hug you, and shower you with affection. I try to make the most of it because those moments are scarce, but I know they are just a step in this journey and I deal with it, knowing one day we will all be reading this together, happy for having our lives back.

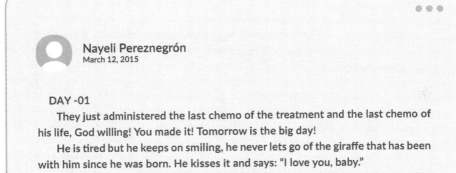

Nayeli Pereznegrón
March 12, 2015

DAY -01

They just administered the last chemo of the treatment and the last chemo of his life, God willing! You made it! Tomorrow is the big day!

He is tired but he keeps on smiling, he never lets go of the giraffe that has been with him since he was born. He kisses it and says: "I love you, baby."

I found out that tomorrow, March 13, is the day of St. Rodrigo Aguilar, namesake of Luis Pablo Aguilar, who was canonized by Pope John Paul II, and who happens to be Mexican. We commend Luis Pablo to him, too.

Thank you, God, for allowing us to get here!

Thank you for your prayers and well wishes! We don't know the exact time of the transplant yet, but it will be done sometime around 10:30 a.m., depending on how long it takes to prepare Luis Pablo and the umbilical cord.

As soon as we know the time, we will let you know so that you can join us in prayer.

👍 9.6 mil 💬 1.3 mil ↗ 444

Luis Aguilar
March 13, 2015

The day is finally here!
Thank God and Virgin Mary for always keeping us by their side.

Today, God has given me the opportunity to experience what I've always believed, that faith can move mountains and that with Him, everything is more manageable.

Luis Pablo is what motivates us to keep going and the biggest example of fortitude, love, and faith. I'm thankful for my wife Naye Pereznegrón and for our families that have always been there for us. I'm also thankful for the love and support of friends and strangers alike.

We will be in this battle for five more years, but we are certain and have faith that everything will be alright. I want to share something that left a mark on me this year: praying for others is a big weapon against any adversity.

As they say: Those who don't learn from their elders, are destined to darkness... and my grandma always used to say: "Never go out without saying a prayer and thanking God." Now I get it.

👍 2.9 mil 💬 1.5 mil ➤ 54

Nayeli Pereznegrón
March 13, 2015

Luis Pablo is having his bone marrow transplant right at this very moment.
Start time: 2:30 p.m. - Mexico, 3:30 p.m. - Houston.

👍 6.8 mil 💬 652 ➤ 26

Nayeli Pereznegrón
March 14, 2015

Day +1

The recovery stage begins now, we're in positive numbers and from now on, everything will be positive. LPAP has been weak but stable, nothing out of the ordinary. Thank you so much for your love and support! Yesterday we could feel some very good vibes during the transplant. From the bottom of our hearts, thank you!

The transplant was done in his room, it's not a surgery, it's more like a transfusion, but just as serious and with medical staff continuously checking his vitals.

Our nurse, another angel, had the great idea of calling someone from the chapel to bless the umbilical cord.

We know God already granted us the miracle, but we have a long way to go during recovery and we continue to ask for your prayers. We still need white blood cells donors for Luis Pablo until his new stem cells engraft and he starts producing his own. This will take between four and six weeks. The following stage is an important one, the new bone marrow must adapt to his body which could potentially cause other complications that I would rather not talk about since I'm sure Luis Pablo won't have those.

In summary: The first 100 days are the most important! It will be over a year of a huge amount of care and complete isolation that will gradually open up. We have no idea when we will be out of this hospital, but since it is such a complicated case, we know it's not going to be anytime soon.

After a year, Luis Pablo will have the immune system of a newborn. We will have to start a whole new immunization schedule and he will still be susceptible to viruses and bacterias.

Somebody asked why my husband said this will be a five year process, the answer is because that's the time frame the doctors give to be officially released. It's a long road, but we don't care because we have the gift of life. You will still be hearing from us. We will still need donors for a few more weeks and we'll need prayers for life: LPAP's life.

Thank you God for letting us witness the power of prayer, it is impressive.

Here's to the miracle baby and the beginning of a whole new life for him!

Nayeli Pereznegrón
March 22, 2015

LPAP is stable and smiling as usual, he's had so much nausea but thank goodness that's the best side effect we could ask for.

He's getting so much medicine that he's thirsty all the time, but he can't hold anything down, so we have to give him water with little sponges, little by little, and even so, he doesn't complain or whines, I admire him more every single day.

He's been weak since he was only able to get two granulocyte donations this week, and he needs those daily. The weather hasn't been nice and we understand that can complicate things, we appreciate your effort, time, and love for our son.

Next week will be better for sure, as always, thank you for your help and donations. As parents, it's so frustrating that my husband is not a match and that they won't let me donate every day. A parent would do anything for their child, but God is blessing us with these angels that have shared their soldiers, cells, and life so that this boy can reach the finish line with no complications. We will be forever grateful for your time, love and support. We're still looking for white blood cell donors. If you can donate, please send a message with the words: POSSIBLE DONOR, your name and phone number to contact you and explain the process.

Once the new marrow "takes" he will start producing white blood cells on his own and we won't need any more donors. We hope this happens as fast as possible, but for now, we still need your help for at least the next two weeks.

His "robot" looks ridiculous with all that medicine. Luis Pablo says he now has the coolest robot with nine heads. Now I'm worried because I told him we will soon have to say goodbye to the robot and that we will be home where he doesn't have to be hooked up to it, he started crying and said the robot was coming home too. When we first arrived at the hospital over a year ago, we had to come up with the story of his friend the "robot" and now he really loves him.

Please keep praying that we have no complications and that everything keeps progressing. Thank you so much!

👍 5.2 mil 💬 336 ➤ 232

Luis Pablo:

Your physical and emotional state are worse than ever since the transplant. Your skin looks gray and it sticks to your bones. You are very skinny, you're swimming in your clothes! But even with all that, you still make the effort to smile. I never thought it would be this hard, everybody told me, but I never imagined all this suffering.

You had blisters and we spent three days treating those. It was horrible to see them filled with blood and watch you tremble when we were treating them. We were being very careful and the dressings were covered in vaseline and medicine, but you don't cry anymore, you just close your eyes and cringe, I believe pain has surpassed your tears.

Doctors keep telling us this is normal, that is why this is the last resort. You are sleeping most of the time and you have good moments, I try to enjoy those at the fullest. When you are sleeping, I talk to you so that you remember that I am by your side, that I love you, and that I need you. I am caring for you with everything that I have. I am so lucky to be able to do this, to be the one who is taking care of this pure soul so full of light.

Your lungs are filled with water so they limited your water intake, we can only give you water with sponges that we put on your lips. You cry in desperation because you want more. I can only take a deep breath and repeat "Jesus, I trust in You" about eighty times. I try to explain that I cannot give you more water, until the doctors say it is okay, and you understand with your kindness and great maturity, you are truly amazing.

Nayeli Pereznegrón
March 30, 2015

Day +17

Hello! I'm sorry I've been gone, I haven't checked my messages... We've hardly left Luis Pablo's side.

On Friday he wasn't feeling well, we almost ended in the ICU again, we were very scared but thank goodness they were able to stabilize him. They had to give him oxygen, we were impressed at his maturity, the first time they did that he was pulling it and crying, this time he understood it was for his own good and he didn't fight it. He is very thirsty but he continues to drink water from a sponge. It breaks my heart that I can't give him water in his sippy cup, when we explained why it has to be this way, he said: "Okay mommy, everything is okay," he grabbed his little sponge, filled it with water and started drinking on his own. These are moments that are engraved in my heart. I admire him so much!

What happened on the weekend was because his new marrow is starting to "take" and it is now producing lymphocytes. LPAP is weak and uncomfortable, but that's normal.

We're all very excited that this is all happening so fast. The umbilical cord transplant can take up to six weeks to engraft, that's longer than a regular transplant. It only took 2 weeks for Luis Pablo's! Which means the new cells are strong. We've been blessed, this is what we were hoping for! We're still waiting, it's a long process, but we're on the right path.

This week we were crushed to learn a little one had passed away.

There are never enough words or right words to say when something like this happens. Please pray for his family. Also, pray for Juanito so that he can soon join us on this transplant floor. He's a warrior!

Don't forget to pray for Luis Pablo, these weeks are crucial! Thank you!

Nayeli Pereznegrón
April 1, 2015

Day +18

Yesterday, Luis Pablo pulled his line and stripped it out. We're waiting for them to take him to the OR and fix it. We've done this so many times that honestly, it feels part of the routine.

Besides this incident, we're still progressing.

At the beginning of the transplant process, in desperation and feeling helpless, we asked the doctors what else could we do as parents. Their answer was something we still remember: "Pray, it is a very complicated case."

Over a year ago, our friends started a prayer chain, then we started this group to find donors during this whole process.

That's when we started writing about Luis Pablo's fight, in response to your support, prayers, and donations. All of you, wanting to know how that little person you've prayed for was doing, the little boy you overcame your fear of needles for.

Our commitment is immense. Our way of thanking God and saying thanks to you for so many prayers and so many donations, will always be by doing something good for others, just like you've done for us many times.

Today we noticed this page has over 25,000 followers. We're so glad that everything we're going through has touched so many hearts, that Luis Pablo's fight has inspired so many to become a better person, to give themselves, to share.

At only two years old, LPAP has added over 50 new people to the bone marrow donor list and he has inspired several mothers in the United States to donate their babies' umbilical cord in Luis Pablo's name. He has gathered over 50 feet of hair donated in his name for cancer patients. He convinced more than 100 people to be blood and platelets donors, and to share those hard to get granulocytes. All of this is thanks to the generosity of the people who follow this journal.

I can't imagine all the things he'll accomplish in his long life ahead.

Thank you for sharing all the beautiful things you do for us, there is not enough time to reply to all, but please know we carry that in our hearts.

Thank you for sharing such personal moments with us, it helps us find a sense in this fight.

As always, please keep praying for Luis Pablo and all the sick children. Let's use these Holy Days to think about the importance of every moment, because every second that goes by is a gift, and we have to enjoy it. God bless you all!

👍 2.2 mil   💬 94   ➤ 54

Nayeli Pereznegrón
5 de abril de 2015

● ● ●

Day +23

Hello! Today is a great day for us, we celebrate the resurrection of Christ that leads us to a path of hope. It doesn't matter the cross we have to carry in our lives, when we decide to carry it with fortitude and conviction that God is awaiting our own resurrection, the load is always lighter. It doesn't matter if we fall like Jesus did, with FAITH we rise up again.

Today, I want to recognize all those moms of children in hospitals that are going or have been through hardship with their kids. We've experienced a real Holy Week, walking by Virgin Mary's side as we see our own child suffer without being able to do anything other than joining them in pain.

Let's remember that today is synonym of HOPE for us too. Happy Easter!

👍 2.4 mil 💬 143 ➤ 54

Luis Pablo,

Today I learned Nathalia went to Heaven. I have been crying since her mom texted to share the news. Even though she told me she was sure Nathalia would be watching over you and that your story would be different, my soul aches, I cannot help but think about her family and the pain they must be feeling right now. I don't understand why life has to be this way for children and such good parents. My mind goes to a dark place and I can't help but think about what could happen to us. I get goosebumps all over my body just to imagine. I can't go on because my tears won't let me, here is what I wrote on social media.

Nayeli Pereznegrón
April 8, 2015

Today, I just want to ask for prayers for the Almanza Beer family.

Nathalia, an angel that we had the privilege of knowing in real life, went to Heaven today. Instead of sharing all the things our kids did while on vacation, here we are, sharing life lessons. Life has changed for us in such a way that we end up being grateful for it. And what most people take for granted, is a privilege for us. Like I've said before, life is simple, and simple things are a blessing.

I'm still speechless. I just want to share a great love lesson in these words written by Arturo: "It won't be in vain, Nathalia has left us with some important life lessons that we must share," a feeling that I understand perfectly, the urge of knowing we're not just doing everyday things, when our everyday will never be the same. LESSONS that go beyond, that are useful.

We are committed for the story to be heard.

With deep love and respect I'm sharing these words written by such a spiritual and remarkable family. LIFE IS SO SIMPLE, AND SIMPLE THINGS ARE A BLESSING.

Fly high Nathalia!!! With your beautiful smile that will forever stay in my heart. Your mom told me today: "She will take care of him, I know it," and I feel the same thing, keep an eye on him, princess. It was an honor to fight this battle along you God and Nathalia have won the battle as they found each other again.

LOVE WINS, IT ALWAYS DOES.

Nathalia Almanza Beer

Nathalia came to this world with a mission and she completed it in less than a year. She taught us the true meaning of life, LOVE. Nathalia spread love everywhere she went and to every person she met. She taught us that the most important thing is family love and unity. She taught us to be strong during the most difficult times. She taught us to have courage in the face of adversity and to never give up no matter what. She taught us to be brave and to fear nothing. She taught us to never complain, but to appreciate life, to always look at the bright side of things, and to be grateful to God for being alive. She taught us that in life everything is possible, and that nothing is impossible. She taught us that in life, you fight until the last moment. She taught us the true meaning of physical, mental, and spiritual strength.

On a personal note, she taught me how to be a dad. I will never forget it and will be forever grateful. She taught me to be a better husband, a better son, a better brother, a better friend, and a better neighbor. She taught me to not be afraid of anything, not even death. She taught me that happiness can be found in the simplest things, and that the most wonderful moments are when we wake up, when we made eye contact and she smiled, when we would feed her, change her, at bedtime, or when we put her in her stroller and went to the park. Happiness is anywhere there's love. She taught me new levels of love that I would've never known. I thought I knew what true love was when I got married and while on our honeymoon, but I was wrong, the love a parent has for their child is a unique kind of love, the most pure and beautiful love there is.

Her passing won't be in vain. Nathalia transcends and gives us life lessons that Miriam and I both feel we need to share with our loved ones. God chose Miriam and me specifically because He saw in us the spiritual and emotional strength needed to pass on these lessons our daughter has taught us. The parent and child love does not end when someone dies, love evolves, I've witnessed that. I was lucky enough to see my daughter be born, grow, smile, eat, crawl, sleep, wake up, dance, sing. I've been blessed by God and I'm thankful to be the father of an angel that had a positive impact on thousands of people.

Please don't feel bad for us, Miriam and I feel blessed and are grateful to God for giving us an angel with such a pure soul. A beautiful light full of love that we enjoyed more than what many other parents do because of the circumstances life gave us. I honestly believe that we wouldn't have learned to love as hard if this hadn't happened. Our souls are hurting because her body is gone and we will miss her terribly, but Nathalia will always be here with us, she will always be in our minds and in our hearts. Nathalia wants her parents to be happy, she wants us to go on and fight for this life just like she did until the last second. Every child wants their parents to be happy and joyful no matter what.

I vow to honor my daughter's memory by trying not to suffer, but to be grateful for all the happy moments, all the smiles she gave us, and every single one of the things we learned. I vow to be happy, to enjoy life like she wants me to do it, to smile constantly and see all the good

in the world. I vow to be strong, to be brave, and to be there for my wife for the rest of my life.

Thank you Nathalia!!!
Rest in peace,
daughter of mine.
The Almanza Beer
Family.

Nayeli Pereznegrón
April 10, 2015

Day +28

LPAP Is getting there, slowly but surely. His numbers went up to 150 early in the week and now they're at a standstill. Any other transplant would be engrafted by now, but ours still has a long road ahead, and that is ok. Here we go, one little step at a time, thank goodness we're not in a hurry.

We continue asking for your prayers so that we stay on the right path. We know God is holding our hand and He won't let go. His new bone marrow is 100% made out of cells from the donor and next week we'll get some very important results that will tell us how the adjustment process is going. We're moving forward, we just have to keep praying for things to continue to do so.

We want to thank Saltillo's newspaper for this moving article they published today. Thanks to the author, Héctor Reyes, for his kind words towards our family, they were a reminder that even when we feel the world is taking over us, a lot of people out there are praying for us and hoping that our life goes back to normal.

Thank you, Ale, for your friendship and for always being there, despite time and distance. I love you. Have a good weekend!

👍 2.3 mil 💬 96 ➤ 50

LUIS PABLO, A TRUE WARRIOR

Their life changed overnight...

Many of us follow Luis Pablo's journey on social media, especially Facebook. A story about a boy from Saltillo that has been fighting a terrible disease for some time now: cancer.

After some tests, this little boy was diagnosed with a silent disease. Instead of being home, right here in Saltillo, he is now spending his days in a hospital in Houston, Texas. His and his family's lives changed overnight.

There is no doubt Luis Pablo has touched many hearts. On a personal note, I first heard about him through my wife Ale, who had the chance of meeting Nayeli and Luis Pablo. The thing that has impacted me the most are the accounts that his mom Nayeli Pereznegrón posts on his Facebook page: LPAP Journal. I am sure more than a few have shed some tears while reading those. But the most impressive thing yet, is the strength of his family, his parents in particular. Quite the example, no doubt.

Luis Pablo has moved thousands of people. People like us, that have never met before, but that with the help of social media are able to share many good stories. For example, we learned that during a marathon, some of the runners were proudly wearing our warrior's initials. This happened in South America.

They say faith can move mountains. Well, today, social media used smartly, can move people.

Every update about the progress of this great little warrior, brings us joy and happiness, and it makes us see that hope can go the distance. Without a doubt, Luis Pablo is an incredible human being that was given a very difficult task. But with God's help, he's overcoming his silent enemy, cancer.

Every time his mom posts something on his Facebook page, we see an impressive amount of likes and comments from people who are attentive to Luis Pablo's well being. It is a true testament of a good use of social media today.

Let's keep on praying for LPAP so that everything keeps moving forward and for the full recovery of our great little warrior. God with Luis Pablo, God with us.

Héctor Reyes
Twitter: @_hreyes

My dearest Luis Pablo,

These have been some hard and boring days. Sometimes this floor drives me crazy, it is always silent, I don't like the vibes, not cool. Every chance I get, I go to the main floor and visit the BE THE MATCH campaign booth, I like to help create awareness among the Latino community, so that people sign up as donors. I also like to share my story, it feels so good to be around people, I miss feeling useful.

Several people asked how to register, and they did! I like to think they did that because of you, and that some day they will give life to somebody.

My beloved child,

I haven't written much because we have been very busy. My heart aches, I know not as much as yours, but it still hurts.

Besides not eating in a long time, you have lost the little muscular strength you had left. You can no longer walk, today they brought us a little wheelchair for you. Your knees are bigger than the rest of your legs, and your belly is larger than your entire body. It hurts me so much to see you like this, and to see how you have lost all of your abilities.

Not only that, little by little you are losing your sight and your hearing, and you stopped talking. It seems like EVERYTHING in you is slowly fading. Your soul understands what is going on and you are so patient with me when you try to tell me something with your eyes. These weeks I have learned how to read your eyes, when something is hurting, when you don't like something, or if you need a hug, the look in your eyes changes.

When you want me to embrace you in a loving hug, the look in your eyes is different. I can't explain it, because your eyes are still so bright all the time, full of life on a dull yellowish body that is so damaged.

I observed you all day today. When you breathe, your belly grows even more, it seems like you are going to explode every time you inhale. You cry without making a sound, tears just run down your face, and my heart is simply broken into a million pieces.

I am still trying to remain positive. I keep smiling and goofing around, but deep down I am just a scared little girl. Never in my life had I known so much love, and I feel so helpless to see it fade away without being able to do anything to stop it. My boy, my only hope is that some day you can understand the love we have for you, and that everything we have done, we did it for you, believe me.

As I have told you a million times before, I would trade places with you without hesitation, but for now, the only thing I can give you is my love and joy, and that is what I try to do every single day. Our love has transcended this world, there is just no way to explain it, it goes beyond words, beyond physical or spiritual… It has become so deep and so pure that I doubt someone can understand it. Our love is something out of this word, along with every paranormal experience we have witnessed and experienced by your side.

Your room in the apartment is ready and waiting for you. I ordered everything online while you were resting. I decorated it with over 50 plush toys that people have sent. You have no idea how excited it makes me just to think about you being out of the hospital. When I go back to the apartment, all e xhausted and heartbroken, I see that room and it r minds me that you will be here soon. Seeing that room gives me hope.

Your room in the apartment is ready and waiting for you.

Nayeli Pereznegrón
April 18, 2015

#LPAP When you're ready... we're ready!!! I'm more excited than when he was going to be born, it finally seems sooner rather than later. Home is where your family is, but I could never call a hospital my home.

👍 1.3 mil   💬 79   ➤ 2

Nayeli Pereznegrón
23 de abril de 2015

Luis Pablo's transplant was a success. Unfortunately, the cancer is back in his new marrow. I'm not going to lie, we're devastated with this news and the pain that we're feeling right now burns us in the deepest part of our souls.

As always, we accept God's will, and we've decided to make him happy every day that He'll let us have him. Because in the end, children are borrowed, and GOD LENT US AN ANGEL and we will always be grateful for that.

LPAP is a miracle already. His fight was a miracle. What he was able to achieve medically is still amazing. My boy is different, he's been special ever since he was born, I knew he was not like the others. He has changed lives, he has transformed hearts, has brought back faith, love and hope to many, many families. HIS FIGHT WAS NOT IN VAIN, and please don't think God didn't grant us the miracle, it's the complete opposite, God is giving us a miracle in a different way.

Today, we understand that God has let us borrow a little angel for two and a half years to complete a great mission. I am so proud and blessed to have been by his side the entire time making him smile, and I will continue to do so until God says so. We are in peace knowing we gave it all and did it all and more, and without a doubt we would do everything all over again.

Luis Pablo has changed our lives for the better, he has taught us to not give up and to be best version of ourselves even in the worst moments.

Luis, my husband, left everything behind to come and live with us, to another country, to give him the best. He was religiously by our side, cheering us up, making us happy. God couldn't have given my child a better father, or given me a better husband. I will be grateful to him my entire life, for not letting us down, for fighting with us with soul and body. Thank you, Luis, for your joy and strength. Thank you for your songs and your music that brightens up our lives. I will always be proud of being your wife and for the way you've embraced this mission. Our commitment is still to give Luis Pablo lots of love and many many smiles, because that's who he is, all love and smiles.

Just before we got the news, Luis Pablo grabbed his PCA Juan's hand (he loves him) and he grabbed my hand, and he started praying by himself: "Our Father, who art in Heaven..." Neither Juan nor I were able to hold back the tears.

When we got the news he asked us: "María, María, María" (a prayer) and right there in front of all the doctors he told me:

"Mom, everything will be alright" and with an enormous peace in my heart, I BELIEVE HIM.

Please keep praying for LPAP and for our family. My husband,

Luis, told me: Right now we need prayers more than ever, and that is true.

PLEASE JOIN LPAP WITH LOTS OF PRAYERS IN THIS LAST BATTLE UNTIL GOD WINS HOWEVER HE WANTS TO WIN IT.

Let's pray that he is always happy!

Thank you to all the staff at the hospital for their excellent attention and the love and care they have given us. You will be a great blessing in our lives forever!

We will carry each and every one of you in our hearts and prayers forever. God has the last say and we will be right here by his side for as long as He says so.

👍 5.3 mil 💬 1.8mil ➤ 981

OUR FINAL DAYS

When a doctor on call came to let us know there was nothing else to do and some other stuff that I cannot remember, I started to feel my body go cold and I fainted. I still cannot remember exactly what happened when I regained consciousness. It seemed like I had lost all my senses.

After I shared the news on social media, I started to think that you might have to leave soon, even though I will keep on begging and believing with all my faith that a miracle can happen. Your dad and I decided to go "home," but it is really an apartment we rented with hopes of bringing you there after your transplant.

At first we said you would stay in the hospital, because honestly, bringing you to the apartment scared me so much, especially having to do everything on my own and suddenly falling asleep because of the physical and emotional exhaustion that I have. We decided that you should spend your last days outside the hospital, not for us, since the hospital would be the easiest thing for us after all this time here, but for you. We believe this is what you would want, and I say "we believe" because as I told you before, you stopped talking a while ago.

Everyone in the hospital was wonderful. They have tried to please us as much as they can, and more. Today, I took an intensive course on how to care for you. I knew how it was done, but now I would have to do it all on my own.

They showed me how to clean your catheter, reminding me of all the precautions I should take, and for the first time they showed me how to prepare your IV fluid and how to hook it up to your catheter. We went over how much vitamin and sugar I should give you through there. After that, they taught us how to give you a shot of morphine, how to prepare it, and how often. We have to guess if you are in pain or not, you usually make an expression showing your pain, and we give you a dose of morphine to ease it. It mortifies me to know you spend most of your days doped. This is when you learn you cannot judge absolutely anyone, because anybody would do anything to stop their children's suffering. I was opposed to giving you morphine, I looked at other more natural options like cannabis oil for pain, but it didn't work.

I had to prove myself because if during my "training" they didn't think I could do it, they would not let us leave the hospital. I gave it my best and was completely focused on not forgetting any detail. I feel a huge responsibility and I am scared of doing something wrong, but I trust that God is helping me like He always has. I know that is true, there is no other way to explain how I have managed to handle so much pain, suffering, and stress, without proper sleep or food for so long. I know He is right there holding me and helping me with his mission.

Your grandparents and aunts haven't left our side, especially now after they heard the news. You know what? I haven't seen them cry.

Maybe they can see how devastated I am and they know I need strength. I feel like I cannot go on anymore.

The support system we have right now is amazing. I truly appreciate it and I am grateful for all the love they are giving us. But, besides that, I am not doing well. I have lost so much weight, I have gastritis and I cannot eat anything. Every bone, every fingernail, every cell in me hurts.

People in this country are planners and very organized.

They always know what to do. That is why today they explained the procedure we should follow after you pass away, what we have to pay, and what we don't have to pay for. We had to decide if we will cremate you or not, if we will bring your body to Mexico or only your ashes. What can I say? It was a horrible day, I would rather forget it.

The only thing I remember is when we went with your godparents to the funeral home. We picked that place only because it was close to the apartment, we didn't even care about prices. I drove by there every time I went to get groceries because it is located right behind the supermarket.

We sat in a gigantic rectangular table that could easily fit 20 people. It was just the four of us and two employees from the funeral home.

"Please," I told them. "Make this fast and easy. I don't want any more torment."

"Of course, ma'am," they replied as they handed me a big pile of paperwork to fill out.

I pushed the papers over to your dad. I couldn't do it. He started talking and asking questions, but I was not listening. I couldn't understand anything, I was not there. Suddenly, I heard: "The urn that will hold his remains" and they pulled out a catalog. When I saw that, my head started pounding as if something heavy had hit it. I started hearing a very high pitch in my ears that wouldn't go away.

"I have to use the restroom," I said.

They brought me to the door. The minute I went in, I started crying. It was the same place that meant so much to me while at the hospital. That corner where so many times I wrote you. I cried, I begged, I got angry, and there I was, one more time in a small bathroom crying and begging God for the strength I needed to remain standing, because if I am being honest, the only thing I want right now is to die and go with you. I cannot bear to imagine the idea of a life without you.

I washed my face, took a deep breath and walked out. When I went back to the table, everybody went quiet and lowered their eyes. I pulled a chair, sat down, and joined them in silence for about half a minute, staring at nothing.

"I don't like any of those urns," I said. "Please tell me the size of the urn needed to hold my son's ashes, who by the way, is still alive."

I said it that way to remind them that I was trying to process something that was inevitably going to happen, but that my son was still waiting for me at the hospital.

"Of course, whatever you wish," they replied respectfully.

"The urn should have these dimensions and hold this many cubic feet."

I wrote that down on my phone and didn't say another word. Your dad took care of everything else. They gave us a phone number and the contact information of the person who would do everything. I didn't show the least amount of interest, this time it was clear that your dad would take the lead.

We left the place. Your godparents were speechless, they could only hug us. I asked them to take me to a pharmacy with a physician on site. I needed to see a doctor, I had a horrible headache and my throat was

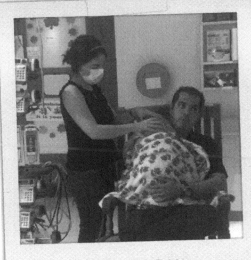

Spoiling Luis Pablo.

166

hurting. I was so worried because being sick meant not being able to be with you.

There, I saw a doctor and I explained my situation. She gave me a shot and told me I would feel better tomorrow, but suggested that I stayed away from the hospital. I didn't tell anybody. I just said I was okay and that I would need a shot at night, which was no big deal in a hospital. There was no way I was going to leave your side. I didn't know how many days you had left and I was not going to waste a single minute. I wore a mask at all times, I made sure to change it every couple of hours and I was constantly washing my hands. I couldn't stay at home "resting" knowing our days are numbered.

While you were sleeping, I looked for urns online. I found one made of marble that you could engrave pictures and words on it. I designed it in 20 minutes. It was a cube, so I put something different on each face. The first one will read: LPAP 2012-2015, the next one will have an angel, another one will have your picture, and the next one will have a picture of the three of us in the ocean. The last one will read: "Forever in our hearts until we meet again. Thank you for so much love. WE LOVE YOU FOREVER."

What else can I say, my boy? With tears in my eyes I am typing that you will probably never read everything I wrote for you… What was the point of doing this? What is the point of going on? Then I discovered this has been my therapy. I looked at you before closing my laptop. I have no more tears to shed, I used them all, I can tell. I hugged you and whispered in your ear: "Ask God to help me be as strong as you."

Nayeli Pereznegrón
May 2, 2015

So many things happened this week. With the help of God and everybody at the hospital, we managed to get LPAP's pain under control, so we were given the green light to go to the apartment. We still have to be close to the hospital, but at least yesterday Luis Pablo was able to be outside for the first time in almost nine months. He saw the cars passing and everything we had prepared for him. He's been so happy at home, he laughed again, he went back to being himself.

As always, we're so grateful with the people at Texas Children's for such a beautiful send-off, it was a nice surprise to see so many familiar faces.
Thanks again to the staff at the 8th floor transplant unit. To the doctors, nurses, and everybody at our beloved floor 9. Thank you to all those people that without speaking Spanish learned our Mexican chant song. We feel so blessed to have so much love.

Yesterday was a gift that will forever stay in our hearts.

Don't forget to pray for us!

👍 5.5 mil   💬 393   ➤ 33

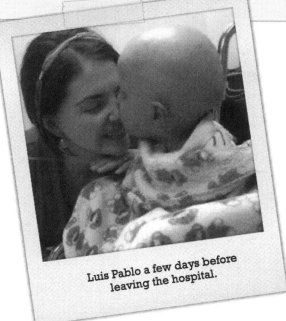

Luis Pablo a few days before
leaving the hospital.

168

After almost nine months, we left the hospital today. I am very excited about your discharge. I dressed you with your nicest shirt, and I made you wear a fancy hat on your bald little head. We prepared your wheelchair and packed everything in the car before leaving.

Juanito, the nurse assistant, came to your room with an enormous balloon. He hugged you tightly and he cried. That is when I came to the realization that the next time we would see him, would be because you would no longer be here. My heart shrunk. I took a deep breath and with a smile I told him: "Thank you for everything, Juanito! You will always be in our prayers."

He couldn't say a word.

My sisters were dressed as Mickey and Pocoyo, ready to walk you to the car and make you happy. We are all so proud of you, of your strength and your determination. Nothing was ever too big for you.

We left our room and we heard cheers and blowout whistles. Streamers and balloons flew through the air. I didn't understand what was happening, I had only planned for my sisters to wear the costumes, but the medical staff, administration, and custodians were waiting for your discharge. The feeling of love and pride was shared throughout the entire hospital.

They lined up on the hallway. They were all cheering for you! I couldn't stop crying, it was such a beautiful gesture. So many people were there, waving goodbye to you. People that I never thought I would see again, and much less right at this moment. People that work at the hospital that I hadn't met before but that follow your story online. Many smiley faces, but with sad eyes. And then, you talked again. Once again, you gave it your best and said goodbye. You were so happy!

I said goodbye to each and everyone of them. I kept thanking them with all of my heart for what they did for us. I will treasure that moment forever.

Your followers on Facebook keep sending us messages. Luis Pablo, you have no idea what they share with us. A person confessed that they tried to commit suicide, but decided to get help after seeing your will to live. You have transformed lives and hearts.

And you did it today, too, with the people at the hospital. You could say they are "used to this" but they were all moved by your fight. It is very clear now that love has no limits and it knows no language or borders. Love is simply love, and you spread love everywhere you go. I am so proud of being the mother of such a special person. I promise you that I will try to be a better person and that I will try to help make other people's lives better, just like you do.

We've been in the apartment for a few days now and things have gone smoothly. I have a thousand alarms and reminders. I haven't missed any of the doses of the more than ten substances you take.

We are quite surprised, and I am even more hopeful for a miracle. You started talking again! Not like before, but you say some words now. It seems that leaving the hospital has helped you and you are getting better. Some volunteers from the Make a Wish foundation visited us today, and they will take us to Disneyland! They suggested May 11 as the date for our trip. We are thrilled! You will finally see Mickey Mouse's house and meet all his friends. I cannot believe we will be together enjoying a trip, you have no idea how happy this makes me. I started to look for matching t-shirts for everybody, but deep inside of me, I feel like you don't really want to go. I keep telling you and you just give me your "no" face. Maybe you are tired, or maybe you don't understand me. I don't know what to think.

We have seen such an improvement that we took you to the zoo today. We rode on a train, but I don't think you really enjoyed it. Even so, you made an effort to spend time with us and make it a special moment.

170

Today, uncle Arturo and auntie Miriam stopped by. I have told you about them before, and about their beautiful daughter, Nathalia, who passed away not too long ago. They hold a very special place in our hearts.

Visit to Houston's zoo.

They brought a machine that looks like something that could be from outer space or from another planet. It looks like a time machine, but it is a machine for energy and electricity, something like that. We did some research and it looks like it is something really good, and we are really grateful for it. They spent the whole day teaching us how to use it.

Right now, my mind is filled with your medicine routine and I cannot remember anything else, so your dad was the one who learned how to use it. Every single night he sits by your side and he starts using the machine giving you those shocks, that is what I call them. It takes about 30 minutes. I am not sure if it helps, but there is no harm in trying. Seeing your dad do that to you in such a loving way fills my heart. I get so moved when I see him praying while he is doing it, asking God for the treatment to work. You have the best dad in the whole entire world, I know that is the reason God trusted him with you.

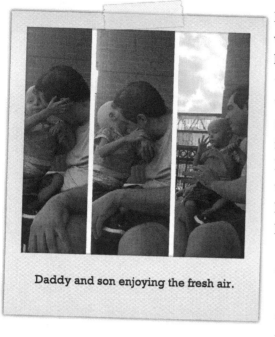

Daddy and son enjoying the fresh air.

It has been four days since we visited the zoo. You don't look good. Your health has worsened so much that, with my deepest sorrow and because of your dad's insistence, we called the Make a Wish Foundation to let them know we would have to postpone our trip to Disneyland. Today is May 7 and we don't believe you will be better in four days.

You are asleep most of the day, that is why whenever you wake up, we all run to your side, to see you, to love you, to tell you how much we love you and how much we want you to be with us. You just smile, ask for water, cuddle with us and in less than 10 minutes you go back to sleep. This has me in low spirits. I have been sleeping next to you, I try to spend as much time with you as possible, I have nothing better to do. I am putting my cheek against your bald little head so often that sometimes it gets wet with sweat. I am going to miss that so much. Sometimes I fall asleep like that and I wake up feeling restless.

I have started to put a finger under your nose again, to check if you are breathing. I did this a million times when you were a newborn. At times, I would see you so calmly asleep, that I was scared you would stop breathing, and that is the exact same feeling I have right now. I also lay my hand on your chest to see if your heart is still beating. I wouldn't want to close my eyes and have you leave us without me being the last thing you see, or without you listening to my voice. I have read so much about that moment that I want to make it as easy as possible, for you

172

at least, because it will never be easy for me. I can tell that day will be here soon, it hurts me and I am afraid.

Today, while you were awake I whispered in your ear: "Luis Pablo, please hang on baby, tomorrow is our 6th wedding anniversary and the next day is Mother's Day, please hang on a little longer, I've never asked anything from you, I would never do it if those weren't such special dates for us."

Medicine time!

Your dad and I barely speak. We get lost on our phones until we hear you talk or cough and we run towards you. I think neither of us wants to talk about it, it is too hard.

Something that has helped us both a bit is a magnet therapy treatment a friend of dad gave us. We have daily sessions and both your dad and I feel very relaxed afterwards. You get treatment too, the therapist tells us you are very strong. That is completely true, you have always showed it.

Luis Pablo, you woke up today and you look great. You have no idea how happy it made us to see you like this, you sang and you cheered, it took some effort but you still did it! But the most amazing thing was that after almost four months of not having any food, you asked for berries! My heart jumped with excitement!

I washed them and I put them in a big bowl in front of you. You started to devour them with joy, just like you would expect from a person that hasn't had any food in four months.

"Mmm… yummy!" you kept saying.

Maybe God will grant us a miracle, son. Maybe you just needed to be out of the hospital. I am sure the magnet therapy and the alternative therapy

Visit to Hermann Park.

machine we got from Miriam and Arturo are working. I don't really know, but the change we noticed in you today is a miracle and nothing more. All that prayer is working.

You asked to go to the park, so I quickly started to get your backpack ready. I got the morphine dispenser, your dad got an IV bag ready just in case, and without thinking, we headed to Hermann Park with your aunt Ale. We rode the train and we enjoyed it so much. It was a great anniversary gift for mommy and daddy to spend the day with the most precious thing our love has brought: YOU! You were feeling so good all day that Ale encouraged us to go out for dinner, just the two of us, to celebrate our anniversary. She offered to babysit. I was not in the mood for going out, much less to dress up, but your dad deserves it. Besides, we could say today was a good day and when there are reasons to celebrate, we mark the occasion! We were celebrating that we found each other, that we are together and that we have overcome so much.

I put on a nice outfit, I did my make up and tried really hard to cover the dark circles under my eyes. I wore some blush to make my cheeks look rosy, and I put black eyeliner to make my eyes look bigger. I hadn't looked at myself in the mirror in a long time. I noticed my eyes were small and swollen and I discovered new wrinkles that I didn't have before. As much as I tried not to focus on my appearance, I still felt ugly and haggard. But the man I was going out with, the same man that stole my heart over six years ago, deserved to go out with a woman that resembled the one he had fallen in love with. So I pumped myself up.

When I came out of the room he looked at me just as I was hoping that he would. He recognized the woman behind all those worries and wrinkles, the one behind a depressed body and a sad look.

"You look beautiful, *chaparrita!*"

"You think?" I blushed as we headed towards the door.

We said goodbye to you, we explained that we would go out to dinner real quick because it was our anniversary. You smiled and with a lot of effort you said the faintest "I love you." We gave you a ton of kisses and told you how much we love you too.

We arrived at our favorite restaurant in Houston, a small place downtown with less than ten tables. The chef is a tall and slender redheaded woman with a personality that projects perfectionism. You can tell from the moment you hear her talk and from the way she pulls the napkin to place it on your lap.

Dinner was delicious. We said we would talk about nice things, we didn't want to talk about your illness. We wanted to pretend nothing was happening. In spite of everything that is going on, we had a very special night together that reminded us of the special kind of love we have for each other, and I must proudly say that it doesn't depend on you, it is the complete opposite, you are the result of that love.

 Nayeli Pereznegrón
May 2, 2015

The last few days have been different. We are still adapting. Being home has been amazing, we've been enjoying our time as a family. We had to learn how to prepare and administer his medication on his central line, and many other nursing tasks. My husband and I have made a good team and we're getting better at it each day. We are committed to enjoy every day with our child, that's why you haven't heard much from us.

As usual, LPAP keeps surprising us. Instead of worsening like he was supposed to, he is getting better. Being home has been good for him, we can tell he is better with each day that goes by and we can't thank God enough for allowing us to do that.

We go to the hospital every other day. And we make the best of the days when we stay home. When he wakes up, the first thing he asks is to go out! He wants to be outside all the time. After 72 days without eating, and when everybody thought he would never eat again, today he tried food again for the first time. As you will see in the video, he was really enjoying it! We are so thankful for such wonderful days!
Please, keep on praying for us!

👍 5.5 mil 💬 393 ➤ 33

 Nayeli Pereznegrón
May 10, 2015

Good morning. Luis Pablo is not doing well today. He is weak and is having trouble breathing. Please pray for him!

👍 3213 💬 500 ➤ 15

Nayeli Pereznegrón
10 de mayo de 2015

• • •

Today, I woke up thinking I would find the same Luis Pablo as yesterday. I even dressed up and put some make up on thinking we could have lunch on the balcony... Once again, it was not the Mother's Day I had hoped for. LPAP has barely been awake since yesterday, they had to come to give him oxygen because of his shallow breathing. But during the short time he was awake, we were able to sit outside on the balcony and he gave me the longest kiss he's ever given me.

Those moments, those short minutes, made my whole day!

Thank you, sis, for capturing the moment!

Thank you God for giving me this moment and for one more day with him! Always in your hands!

Thank you, Pavito, for making me a mom for the first time and forever! Thank you for giving me so much love and for this wonderful amazing week! You always do your best, my little angel! I love you with all my heart. And, how does my heart beat for you?

👍 3213   💬 500   ↗ 15

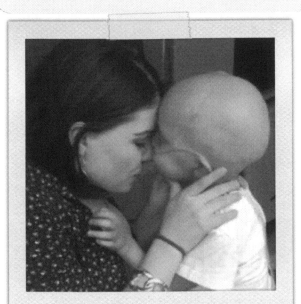

**Nayeli and Luis Pablo
celebrating Mothers' Day.**

177

After posting that on Facebook I called the doctor who was overseeing your bone marrow transplant. I told her you were not looking good, that you had trouble breathing and that I thought we should take you to the hospital. I started crying as I was talking to her, I couldn't help it.

"Okay, I understand you're renting an apartment not too far from the hospital, right?" She asked.

"Yes," I managed to reply as a lump formed in my throat.

"What's the address? I will stop by to check on him. I wouldn't want you to spend Mother's Day at the hospital if it isn't necessary."

I quickly shared my location with her and I started to pack our bags. I wanted to have everything ready before she arrived because I knew we would have to go to the hospital. That's how bad you seemed.

I went into your room and as I held you, I begged you to stay with me, but you were not waking up. I was not even sure you were listening, but something inside me needed to talk to you.

"Luis Pablo, I only want you to be happy my love, I've never asked you to do anything for me, but today, I have to. Please, be strong, hang on a little longer. Today is Mother's Day. If you stop fighting just today, it would be a day of unbearable pain for me. Forever. I could never again celebrate being a mother without thinking that somehow, on this same day, I stopped being one."

"Please my baby, please," I kept saying over and over again, crying and hoping you could hear me, as I was holding a completely unresponsive child.

The door rang.

"The doctor is here!" I yelled.

You opened your eyes.

She came in and as I greeted her, I told her you were not doing well at all.

But then, I heard your voice in the background.

"It seems like he just woke up," I told her. "But he's not doing well." We walked into your room and you were playing with a toy car and asking Ale to pass you some other things to play with. "Look mom! Vroom!"

It had been so long since I heard your voice so loud and clear. My eyes couldn't believe what I was seeing. I turned to look at your dad and he couldn't believe it either.

"Well, he looks good to me," the doctor said.

My face started to turn red. I was so embarrassed! The doctor was so busy and I had made her leave the hospital to come check on a child that could pass for a perfectly healthy boy right at that moment.

"Cari, I swear he was not like this," your dad told the doctor. "I don't know how to explain it, he was not responsive."

I backed him up immediately while she carefully listened to your breathing and checked your pulse.

"His levels are fine. Don't worry, you can stay home, there is nothing to be worried about. Enjoy your day, Nayeli. Give him a lot of hugs."

"Doctor, thank you so much for coming, it means a lot to us. And again, so sorry! Seriously, he seems like a totally different kid," I told her.

"Don't worry about it, I'm happy to do it."

Your dad walked her to the door as I remained perplexed at what was happening. I hugged you.

"You little rascal! You put me on the spot! But I don't mind if it means I get to see you like this!" I told you as I showered you with kisses and we started playing.

I really enjoyed that moment, I never wanted it to end. But about half an hour later, you started to get tired and you asked to go to sleep.

Something happened that day that exhaustion took over us. I was drained. I needed to rest and so did your aunt Ale, who suggested the nurse took care of you that night. Your dad agreed with the idea and convinced us to get some rest that night, and as unbelievable as it sounds, that night we all slept like a log.

I have to confess that in my sleep I could hear you calling me, "Mommy, come." I don't know if I was dreaming, if I made it up, or if it was really you, but my body could not react. I tried to get up but I couldn't do it, it was as if something very heavy was holding me down and wouldn't let me wake up. My grandma would say that "the witch was riding my back," but I just call it extreme fatigue.

⌁♡2⌁

May 11

I woke up at 7 a.m. and ran to see you. You were talking to the nurse, and the moment you saw me, you said: "Hi mom!"

"My darling boy! Let's go to the hospital" I said as I was getting ready to leave.

You had an appointment for a blood and platelets transfusion. Dad offered to take you so that I could take a shower.

I accepted his offer. I really wanted to take a shower with very hot water without being in a rush, and I did. At around 10 in the morning, I headed to the hospital. Your aunt Ale was still asleep so I left a note that read: "We went to the hospital to get LP his platelets. Meet us there when you're ready."

Since it was a long process, we all knew there was no rush. When I arrived to your room, you were asleep and you were having trouble breathing.

"What happened? How is he doing?" I asked your dad.

"Well, the same," he answered.

"Go get something to eat, I already had breakfast, I'll stay with him." And he left.

Something was not right. I could tell something was different.

The staff at the hospital seemed more worried than usual. Nobody was saying anything. They would only come in, check your vitals, and leave. As they passed me by, the nurses would smile at me, but it was not a courtesy smile. This time, it was different.

The charge nurse from the floor came in and she greeted me with the biggest smile.

"Good morning, could I see his lab results from today?" I asked.

Her expression went from happy to nervous, but she agreed to bring me a copy.

Five long minutes went by. I could see how your stomach would grow every time you struggled to take a breath.

The nurse came back with the results and I went over them. Zero neutrophils as usual. Your hemoglobin was very low but they had given you some already, so I was not worried about that. But then, something stood out: Carbon Dioxide.

My mind went still for a minute trying to remember all the books I had read. My brain started to spin as I went over every cancer-related book I had ever looked up. The nurse stood there without saying a word. She was waiting for me to finish going through the results, as if she was waiting for me to say something.

I kept thinking for about two minutes. Then, my eyes started to fill up with tears until I could no longer see the paper I was reading. I turned to the nurse, whose eyes were as teary as mine.

"Is he going?"

"Yes," she replied as she stared at the floor.

A long silence took over the room, until we heard your voice asking for water.

I turned to see the nurse waiting for her approval.

"Go ahead, just try not to give him much because of what could happen."

She then walked towards you. She was crying but she kept on smiling.

"Oh, Luis Pablo! You have no idea how much we love you around here." And you, with great effort, put your hands on her face, and with a weak voice told her: "Don't cry, everything will be alright." I wish I had captured this moment in a picture.

Holding back my tears, I translated for her.

"You are so right, my boy. Everything is going to be alright," she said as she kissed and hugged you tightly.

I called your father. In the meantime, I held you and I put on a song from a singer called Rosana. I tried singing to you but I couldn't stop crying:

> *No habrá nadie que te quiera más que yo*
> *Dentro y fuera de esta tierra como yo*
> *Puede ser que no lo veas o tal vez que no lo creas*
> *Bien lo sabe Dios que en el mundo del amor...*
> *(There will be no one that loves you more than me*
> *In or out of this world, like me*
> *You might not see it or you might not believe it*
> *But God know that when it comes about love...)*

Then, you said: *"Mi cachito,"* and as I was weeping, I sang the verse I had adapted for you:

> *You always pretend you are super Pocoyo,*
> *And that you fly with Peppa Pig on a train,*
> *that you fight against the bad guys and you beat them too,*
> *You always win, you never like to lose.*
> Patty Ibarra de León.

I started to feel very anxious. I grabbed my phone and posted:

Nayeli Pereznegrón
May 11, 2015

Luis Pablo was admitted to the hospital again. He is in critical condition. Please, we are asking to pray for him and for us. May God's will be done, because his will is always the best for us. Please, keep on praying that he is stabilized and without pain.

👍 3213   💬 500   ➤ 15

I couldn't stop thinking that today was supposed to be the day we left for our Disneyland trip. I was so glad I listened to your dad and we didn't go.

Your dad was back in the room after a few minutes, but it seemed like hours to me.

"Daddy, daddy!" You kept saying, over and over again.

When he got there, he ran to hug you while I explained everything that was happening. Your doctor came too, without saying anything, she just hugged us, and then she said they were already getting a room ready for us, so that we could be more comfortable.

"*Pavo*, your grandparents are coming to see you! *Tata, Tita, Nana, Abu, Tati*... they are are all on their way!"

"No mom, tell them bye, bye."

You didn't want to see anyone, you were feeling that bad. Your godmother, Ale, arrived at the same time as your dad but she stayed in a corner without making a sound. When she noticed us going through some papers, with tears in her eyes she walked over to your side, kissed you, and gave you a loving hug. You touched her face, as if you were saying goodbye. She cried and told you she loved you, then she went back to the corner. I watched everything happening in slow motion.

"No. Bye, bye," you struggled to say.

"What is going on, *Pavo*?" We asked you as we came to your side.

"Bye, bye, bye, bye," you kept saying, agitated, looking towards the door. I felt chills. I had no idea what you were looking at, but I wanted you to feel safe even if I didn't understand.

"OUT, OUT!" you started yelling in distress, as you kept trying to leave your bed.

"Everything is going to be alright, you can rest now, baby, we promise we will be fine. Over there, your other grandpa is waiting for you, along with your namesake Juan Pablo, and Jesus, and Mary."

"I don't want to, mommy, bye," you said again.

"*Pavo*, tell them it's okay, they are here for you, it's time to go."

"I don't want to mommy, I don't want to…"

I started to cry uncontrollably but I was still trying to keep talking to you.

"Yay, *Pavo*! It's so cool! You are now going to run on gardens, and you are going to jump, and nothing is going to hurt anymore, nothing! Can you imagine?" I told you, bawling but with a big smile.

I felt more and more pain with each word that came out of my mouth, but I had to do it. You couldn't take any more suffering and we had to help you. I felt it was my duty to make you feel safe and to try to make you happy, up until your last breath. I would deal with myself later.

You kept looking at the door. You wouldn't stop staring at it, even as I was talking to you.

"You know what?" I told you, "I'm going to get there really soon! When you least expect it, I will be there with you. Find the most beautiful garden, like the ones we like so much, filled with flowers and lakes, and when I get there, you can show it to me, okay?"

Then, you turned to me with your tired eyes, and said:

"Okay, but you come."

My heart finished shattering into a billion pieces. I really wished with my whole entire soul to go with you. Wherever that was. I didn't care. I just wanted to protect you, to hug you, to not let you go.

"Yes my love, I will go there too, but not today. There are still a lot of people that I need to help, you already did enough and we are so proud of you."

Your dad, who couldn't stop crying came closer to you.

"Yes, my son, we are so very proud of you, *Pavito*. I love you my baby," he told you. "So cool that you are going to see Jesus and Mary, please say hi to my dad for me when you see him."

You made a huge effort to touch his cheeks, you were more weak by the minute and you were struggling more and more to catch your breath.

Your nurse and doctor came to check on your machines and to let us know our room was ready. Your dad asked Ale to please bring his guitar from the apartment. He wanted to sing for you. Ale said yes. I was still seeing how you struggled to breathe.

When I turned my eyes to look at Ale, I watched as her expression changed completely. I quickly turned to look at you... You had stopped breathing!

I let out a harrowing cry.

Your dad turned and ran towards you with a face that I will never be able to erase from my head. It was an expression of uncertainty, helplessness, and pain.

"Did it already happen?" Your dad asked.

"Calm down," the doctor told me. "Calm down Nayeli," she continued to say as the crying nurse was removing your oxygen tank and turning off the machines.

Dad started to pray nonstop, and I suddenly remembered I had once read that the last sense a person loses when they are dying is their hearing.

I told your father and I started talking.

"I love you, *Pavo*, thank you for everything you did for me, keep on being happy."

My last words for you were:

"When you're by God's side, please ask him to look after my heart."

I went to a corner to cry. My heart was aching like never before. It was burning, I could feel it, I couldn't breathe. Your father said his goodbyes too and started to talk to the doctor.

Until after dad left your side, Ale kissed and hugged you. The news spread quickly around the hospital. The first one to arrive was our beloved.

Dr. George, he hugged us and cried, too.

"Is it okay if I hug him?" He asked.

"Of course Doc, you're like family," I replied.

And with tears in his eyes he stood by your side.

"Goodbye. Thank you, Luis Pablo," he told you as he kissed you.

Your oncologist quickly followed. She didn't say a word, she just hugged us tightly, and then went over to kiss your forehead and told you that she loved you.

I was still in my corner, crying and trying to process what was happening, trying to catch my breath.

I looked at you but you were no longer there, I could tell. It is something that I will never be able to explain, but I felt as if you had already left, your dad felt it too. I covered you with a bedsheet as I said: "I want to remember my happy *Pavo*, he was always happy."

The hospital staff came one by one to offer their condolences.

After a while, I was feeling a little calmer and I told your dad we should leave. He agreed. Your doctor asked if we wanted to wait until they picked you up.

"He's no longer here," I answered.

"Okay, as you wish," she said.

"Please, just make sure they take his blanket and his baby giraffe."

I had asked them to cremate you with them.

"Of course," the doctor said, and she hugged us.

As we were leaving, your doctor called our names.

"Wait! His stroller and diaper bag!"

"No doctor, I came here with my son, and I am leaving without him and without his stuff. Those things are staying here, donate them or do whatever you want with them," I said.

"Understood."

We opened the curtains and all the staff of the transplant floor pretended they were not watching. They were staring at their computers and their phones. I noticed most of them had teary eyes.

"Thank you all, for everything," your dad said.

A lot of them started crying and formed a line to hug us. Among all those hugs and so many "I'm sorry", somebody told me:
"What you're going through is awful and extremely hard, but your husband is also going through the same thing, don't push him away, let him be your shelter, think about him, too. Over half of the couples that go through something like this end up divorcing."

I still can't conceive why they would tell me that. My mind couldn't manage to think about another loss after I had just experienced the biggest loss of my life.

On our way to the apartment, once again I started to think how we were supposed to go to Disneyland. Today was supposed to be a magical day, but you had gone on a trip that I was not invited to.

Back in the apartment, I remember that I went into your room where everything was just as we had left it a few hours before. I locked myself in there. I hugged your plush toys and cried until I fell asleep.

I woke up because my cellphone was ringing. It was my father calling to let me know they had arrived at the airport.

"Head over to the apartment, dad, Luis Pablo got better and we came here."

"See! I told you! Our little Pavo just wanted to see us," I overheard my mom say.

"Let me know when you arrive to let you in," I said before hanging up.

After 45 minutes, I got their call. I went down the elevator and when the doors opened, everybody was there waiting for me.

"How is he doing, Naye?" My mom asked before greeting me.

"Family, Luis Pablo is already in Heaven."

I watched as each one of them changed the expression on their faces. They all walked in different directions. They were all crying. After a moment, my mom hugged me.

"How are you doing, sweetheart?" she asked.

"I'm okay."

We headed upstairs. We told them everything and asked them not to say anything yet since we were still waiting for your dad's family to arrive the next day. We didn't want them to be upset on their flight here. We were always thinking of them.

Your grandparents and aunts went to their hotel.

After dad and I talked, cried, and made plans, we fell into a deep continuous sleep.

The next day, I woke up at the same exact time as always. I did what I would always do, and I grabbed the car keys.

"Where are you going?" Your dad asked surprised.

"I'm going to the hospital," I replied.

He looked at me as if I was crazy.

"Naye, why do you want to go to the hospital?"

I lowered my head and stared at the floor as I was trying to find a valid reason, but I couldn't find an explanation.

"I don't know, but I want to go," I said before I headed towards the door and left.

In the car, I studied the road. I wanted everything etched in my memory. Every street, every shopping center, every store near the hospital, the street filled with oak trees that we liked so much. When I got to the hospital, I parked right in front of what used to be your room, and I started crying. I was crying because I could no longer feel you, and I wanted to feel you. I was so desperate to feel your presence somehow. Maybe my mind thought doing this would help, but it didn't. I felt alone, utterly and completely alone. You were my entire life and you are no longer here.

I love you with all my heart, *Pavo*!

And now… How will my heart beat without you?

Nayeli Pereznegrón
May 12, 2015

God and LPAP had won their battle against cancer, and in recognition, Luis Pablo has earned a big beautiful pair of wings. His heart stopped beating yesterday, May 11 at 3:40 p.m. Our hero is now our angel.

Thousands of us are mourning your departure, but your enormous legacy will stay in our hearts forever. I am certain that thousands of angels greeted you warmly over there, cheering for you like you asked us to do until your last minutes, they must be so happy to have you back there.

Thank you God! For allowing me to be by his side up until his last breath. With all my heart I wanted you to spend Mother's Day with me, and you made it happen.

We couldn't take you to Disney, but I'm sure you're in a much better place!

Today, you're finally a healthy child! Today, you're running in the sky without any cables, without medicines, and without any pain.

We are in peace knowing that when you arrive, you will recognize Jesus, Mary and Pope John Paul II, we made sure you knew about them since you were born.

We want you all to know that he fought until the end, up until his last moments he was still asking to go out, we calmly told him: "Everything will be alright, you can rest now, son, we promise you we will be fine, your grandpa (my father in-law) is waiting to meet you over there, as well as your namesake John Paul II (you're named after him), and Jesus, and Mary."

I've always believed that families that go through something as painful as losing a child, will have a reward in eternal life.

Ours will be to have our little two-and-a-half-year old, forever in eternity.

I will never forget how you used to say: "Everything will be alright" and with your eyes you were begging us to believe you. Amidst the most awful pain you were always smiling, we promise to honor you by doing the same. We will try to enjoy every day with a smile, no matter what, just like you did. I personally, promise you to take care of dad's heart, and to make him very happy so that the three of us can continue to live together, just how you liked it, but now, it will be forever.

You are a miracle that will be living in our hearts forever, until we are able to hug you again.

You fought like no other warrior, Luis Pablo! I am so very proud of you and we are so privileged to be your parents in this world. Our lives will never be the same because of you, from now on, WE WILL TRULY LIVE. Thank you for showing us the most pureand selfless kind of love.

Putting our lives back together is going to be very hard without you, but with yours and God's help, I have no doubt we will make it.

We will miss you every day for the rest of our lives, but we will be okay, for you and because of you.

Don't forget about our picnic at the park, my Pavito! Find the most beautiful one you can find in Heaven so that you can take me when I get there!

See you then my beautiful smiling angel, we love you with all of our hearts!

And how do our hearts beat for you?

👍 3213   💬 500   ➤ 15

LIFE AFTER YOU

After we announced your departure, we received nonstop calls, messages, gifts, and displays of affection. From the moment we got off the plane, a gift from a family we love very much, to attend the Masses offered for you in Saltillo, the staff at the airport greeted us with flowers. There was food in our house, gifts, flower arrangements, it was unbelievable. We even got a letter and some flowers from the city's mayor. All the love and solidarity we received was overwhelming.

Religious funeral service

A lot of people attended your service. So many that my jaw started hurting. I remembered the same thing happened on my wedding day, seeing so many familiar faces and some others that I didn't know. Both times, the churches were completely full, there were even people standing in the atrium.

The Masses were perfect, better than what I could have imagined. The church was filled with with colorful balloons of all sizes, just like the ones you liked. At the end of the ceremony, we released those balloons into the sky with applauses and the loudest cheer. Everybody kept clapping, crying and smiling at the same time. The terrace outside Our Lady of Fatima's church was full of color and full of people that were celebrating the fact that they knew you, because you touched more lives than I could ever imagine.

People dressed in white holding a candle were lined up along the way to where we would inter your ashes, this was something that moved me deeply. I didn't know most of the faces, but they were there, without having met you, crying and sharing our pain, touched by you.

To our surprise, when we released the balloons, the clouds in the sky took the shape of a gigantic heart with wings.

Everybody was taking pictures of it. To me, this was the answer to my question: "How is my heart going to beat without you?" And also, to my request: "Ask God to look after my heart." Seeing that heart in the sky meant you were there, and it was what I had asked you for every night since you left, for a signal that would let me know everything was going to be all right.

The sign that everything is going to be all right.

I have decided that from now on, I will fight the worst cancer of all, the cancer that attacks the souls. I will conquer this in your honor. I know it, because I know you are here with me, in a completely different way, but still, I know you will be the one who will take care of me, you will be the one who dresses my wounds, and the one who will hug me when it hurts.

Nayeli Pereznegrón
May 21, 2015

We would like to give a special thanks to all of you who joined us with their prayers, Masses, sacrifices, good vibes, and many other nice gestures you all did for us during these past 18 months.

Thank you to the over 200 donors that gifted him life, and to all of those that were in the process of doing so. Something characteristic of Luis Pablo was that he was very grateful, I'm sure that he will be watching over you from the sky, because he took a little piece of you with him.

Thanks to our family and friends for all their love and support, especially to those in charge of organizing Luis Pablo's Masses.

Thank you for allowing us to enjoy the moment without having to worry about planning anything. Thank you for taking care of every single thing, you even made sure we arrived in Saltillo, we couldn't have done it better, we didn't have the head for it!

Thank you, Father Chuy Pedro and Father Pío for such beautiful services. Thank you to the chorus for singing beautifully and who didn't want to charge us anything. May God pay you back with many, many blessings.

Thank you to all of those who were there with us. Thank you for all the food and desserts you brought to our house, thank you for the flowers and the many details. Thank you for the favors that were handed out. Thank you for so much love for our little boy.

I've decided to temporarily close my Facebook account because I have 1751 private messages on my personal account, and over 2100 on LPAP Journal's page. There are close to 4000 messages that are making everything crash, we must have done something good in order to receive all this love, but our capacity is very limited and it's hard to keep up. We will try to read everything and respond little by little, but for now I would like to offer my most sincere gratitude to each and every single one of you that have written or have joined us here.

The best way to join Luis and me to honor Luis Pablo is by practicing as little or as much as we have passed on to you, and that together (just as we've done before) we can continue helping other children by bringing them positive experiences as the great community we formed these last two years. Let's make sure that other people's suffering doesn't come and go before our eyes.

I'm not a psychologist and I'm not pretending to be one, I've never even been to one. I simply love life, I am a true believer of the lessons that it teaches us, and I try to be grateful for it.

The past is in the past, and we'll keep the happy moments. LPAP will always be a great treasure we will carry in our hearts, and that we will never stop missing, but we don't want to meet him again one day and bring him a package full of tears, sorrows, and negative things after he left. It would make no sense to have instilled in him all that joy, and happiness, and love for life, and then do the opposite thing. This is how we've decided to honor him. We know this is how he wants to be remembered.

Our mission as Luis Pablo's parents is just starting, the lessons we learned will not stay in our hearts and heads. After taking some time for myself, to experience the things I have to live, I will come back to think and put forward some proposals, I will work in whatever God wants me to, and however He thinks I would be of help, being at his disposal as I've always been.

Our commitment in appreciation for all the help we received during this time, we will be helping other kids like Luis Pablo, when the time is right. When Luis Pablo was first diagnosed, we went through our mourning process, but even then, we woke up every single day and made the choice to be happy. Even when the prognosis was not looking good, we had two options:

1. Feel sorry for ourselves, stop fighting, get bitter and cry all the time as we saw other families do.

2. Fight for his life and be happy, even if the circumstances were not ideal, and seek shelter in God.

You experienced our choice along with us for almost two years, and that choice hasn't changed. We are lucky to say that when we think of Luis Pablo, we do it with the biggest smile. We enjoyed every day with our son as if it was the last one, we gave him everything we could, we did our best, we were fully devoted to him.

We left no what-ifs. There are no regrets. And when you are blessed to be able to say goodbye to your child this way, while being so close to God, you have the satisfaction of knowing you've fulfilled your duty, and that is the biggest blessing.

We are sad because we don't get to see him anytime soon, but happy because of the special relationship we had with him, and because nothing was left to be said. There's no guilt, there was only love.

We're living our grief as a couple, as we've decided we want to grieve. In the end, nobody will understand what I went through better than my husband, and vice versa. I couldn't even say that I know what a mother that went through the same thing is feeling, because the experiences and situations are always different. I would be lacking humbleness to say that because I already went through that, I know what that person is experiencing, when the truth is that I have no idea.

I must say that we can never imagine or feel something we are not experiencing. I had two weeks to prepare after they declared my son terminally ill. I thought I could imagine what I was going to feel, I thought I was prepared for that, and I was so arrogant to pretend I could even imagine it. Reality and imagination are opposites, we will never be ready for that, we will never know what it's like until it happens.

That's why we decided to be together, the only two people that can understand what the other is going through right now, us, the parents, and away from everything, in contact with nature because we were shut away in a hospital for a long time. We are mourning a great loss, but grateful for the life we have ahead of us, the world that we're yet to discover. We are learning that our relationship with Luis Pablo will be similar to the one we have with God, we cannot see him or touch him, but that doesn't stop us from feeling him very close to us.

Life is here, we have it today but can't be certain that we will have it tomorrow, how we live our lives is our choice. We have decided to go on and enjoy the time God grants us in this world!

Thank you for showing your solidarity to us this way.

With love, respect, and the deepest gratitude,
The Aguilar Pereznegrón family.

👍 9.5 mil 💬 883 ➤ 301

Luchando Por Ángeles Pequeños "LPAP" (Fighting for Little Angels) was officially started on October 29, 2015, the day of Luis Pablo's birthday. A party was held in his honor to collect gifts for children with cancer. Over 90% of the birthday party was donated by people from Saltillo that wanted to help. The event was organized by Nayeli's family and friends.

Luis, Naye, Mickey, and Minnie cut the ribbon at the opening ceremony, joined by all of Luis Pablo's friends and the costumes that were with him during his hospital stay.

In the five years since it started operations, LPAP has created eleven programs to help low-income children who are battling leukemia. Some of these programs are inspired by the ones that helped them while in Houston, like the one that decorates the patients' rooms, the one that fulfills the family's Christmas list, and the one that provides families with groceries and basic necessities every month.

Opening day for Luchando por Ángeles Pequeños.

Other programs were created according to the needs they found in hospitals in Mexico, such as covering chemotherapy costs, funeral expenses, and fees that no insurance would cover for a bone barrow transplant.

To this day, they have helped over 600 boys and girls. Nayeli always says that helping is very rewarding for Luis and

196

for her. Knowing that several little ones are still alive because of these programs, lessens the pain they feel when thinking that their son couldn't make it.

The foundation covers a monthly transportation fee for patients that live far from where they receive treatment. This has ensured that over 100 children continue their chemotherapy treatment.

LPAP A.C. has earned a transparency certification from the Mexican Center for Philanthropy: CEMEFI.

Nayeli and her husband volunteer for this cause, which they call "their son's legacy" and, along with their families, they cover the foundation's operating expenses so that 100% of the external donations can reach those families in need.

Nayeli states that all of this is possible because of God, Virgin Mary, Luis Pablo, her team, and people that join the cause motivated by love; people that, in her own words, are sent by God.

Two months after Luis Pablo's departure, the director of LPAP delivered her first speech to an audience full of children, according to her, this has been her toughest audience. To this day, she has given over 50 talks in different states in Mexico, all of them in benefit of the foundation.

Around 90% of the donations made to LPAP come from

the same social media platforms that helped their child, and from the projects and events they organize to generate income, among those, this book.

The motto of the foundation is: "The sky is our limit, and over there we have angels fighting with us too."

"When my son left this world and went to Heaven, I stopped feeling him, I stopped feeling God and my son, so I spent some time looking for them, and because everything is part of a perfect plan, while I was trying to find them… I ended up finding myself."

If you would like to support or know more about Luchando por Ángeles Pequeños you can do it on their website:

www.lpap.com.mx and social media:

f   LPAP A.C. Luchando Por Ángeles Pequeños

🅞   luchandoporangelespequeños

🐦   FUNDACION LPAP @LPAP

Paypal - www.paypal.me/lpap2020

Shortly after the Masses offered for my son, my husband and I took a long trip. There, we found ourselves again after so much time apart when the only thing we would talk about was, of course, Luis Pablo, who by the way made himself present the entire time.

A few months after that, I traveled to Calcutta, India, with my sisters and two of my closest friends who were always by my side. In many of my posts I shared my admiration for Mother Teresa of Calcutta, being in her home, knowing her environment, and seeing what she created, helped me greatly.

Being a missionary of charity has been one of the most gratifying experiences of my life. I was looking everywhere for signs, and my answers were always "give thanks" and that's what I did. I came back from that trip being grateful and realizing that besides everything we went through, we were lucky. We were in a good hospital that provided great care, and we had every service available for our son.

I couldn't complain, I had no right to after everything I saw during that life-changing trip where I learned that everything is a grace, including the loss of a child.

After dealing with some medical issues that were the result of all the stress and not taking good care of myself while caring for my son, on May 9 of 2016, as an anniversary gift, we found out we were pregnant. We didn't want to say anything because two days later we would offer a Mass for the first anniversary of Luis Pablo's passing. We didn't want anybody to congratulate us at church that day, but still, he made sure that I didn't spend one single Mother's Day alone. That day, besides missing him terribly, I knew that there was a little person growing inside me, and I tried to stay positive because it was no longer me alone, we were us again.

Bosco was born a day before Christmas, again, Luis Pablo made sure we didn't spend one Christmas without truly celebrating. Bosco is our rainbow baby, those of you who follow me on social media know that he came to this world to make us laugh our hearts out. He is an incredible loving child, he is pure sweetness, and he has the biggest heart.

Four months after Bosco was born, we found out a girl was on her way to add a touch of pink to our lives, Luisa. She came here to complement our family with a dose of tenderness, mischief, and joy like no other. She has the same temperament as Luis Pablo, and she makes us think of him even more. Luisa, by the way, was born on March 28, close to the date of Luis Pablo's transplant when we begged so hard for a child's life.

I always say that my heart is scared for life. It is like when someone has their legs amputated, they will never get them back, but they learn to live without them, they learn to live in a different way, they learn how to use a wheelchair, and if they want, they can smile again and enjoy their new life. Well, to me, my soul was amputated and I have learned to live like that, without any hitches to be happy. The only advise I can give you to achieve this: GOD.

In our family, Luis Pablo is always present. From the moment our day begins and until it ends. My children know him perfectly well and they include him in every sibling conversation. It is impossible to erase from our family someone who brought us so much, besides he constantly reminds us that he is among us.

Our lives changed completely. There is a definite before and after Luis Pablo. Now, we enjoy everything, the little things and also the big ones without any remorse. He makes us want to be better people.

Today, his life will continue to touch as many hearts as God wants through this book... his book. Thank you for being a part of our story.

The Aguilar Pereznegrón family.

ABOUT THE AUTHOR

Nayeli Pereznegrón Galindo

Wife and mother of three, she is a Lawyer, human rights and social activist, and holds a degree in International Law.

Nayeli has worked with several publications as a writer and editorial advisor. Her column 'Todo Va a Estar Bien' has been published in several local newspapers, and has been featured national and internationally.

After her son Luis Pablo went to Heaven, she and her husband started 'Luchando por Ángeles Pequeños A.C.', a foundation that helps children from lower-income families in México who are battling cancer. As president of this foundation, she has given many talks, served as an advisor for local and state programs, and has been awarded many honors.

She currently resides in Saltillo, MX with her husband and their two children, as they continue to grow their firstborn son's legacy.

www.nayelipereznegron.com